T0306129

Health and Safety Leadership Strategy

The purpose of this book is to awaken leaders to the unique opportunities now present in the areas typically delegated to Health and Safety. It is a strategy to utilize existing resources to fully develop and engage human potential to catapult business achievement. The confluence of Covid-19, the resulting burnout, the attention on diversity, equity and inclusion generated by the Black Lives Matter movement and the 'great resignation' continues to create openings to fundamentally change how we address personal development, sustainable growth and social responsibility. The argument within is that the better we manage the social aspects of the organization, the better our business results.

Elucidating to the reader the societal shifts of workplace culture in recent years, this text expertly analyzes the importance of mental health in the workplace, whilst also explaining how management and HR departments can improve. It examines who is responsible for generating psychological safety and provides relationship strategies that will improve performance. The critiques in this text establish why it is imperative for business leaders to concentrate on how their company culture affects their employees, and whether their employees feel safe, seen and supported. The concepts and practices in this book are the ones that leaders have used across the ages to create commitment, accountability and excellence. Managers will benefit from a deeper understanding of how these issues impact every aspect of organizational performance.

This book is essential reading for executives, leaders and those interested in leadership. They could be in the C-suite, operations, health and safety and HR. It is also directly relevant to organization development and change management specialists interested in including safety within their practice.

Rosa Antonia Carrillo, president of Carrillo and Associates, is an internationally recognized leader in creating transformational change with a focus on the safety, environment and health function. Since 1995 she has authored ground-breaking articles in the safety field and consulted in many countries across multiple industries on the topic of safety leadership. Edgar H. Schein recommended her book *The Relationship Factor in Safety Leadership* as required reading for anyone wanting to understand safety culture.

"This is an important book detailing the core principles of organizational development state of the practice. As Carrillo correctly points out, the Covid-19 pandemic was a global event that cracked the barrier to significant systemic change. Moreover, we are still experiencing the changes from psychological 'languishing' to 'laying flat' and the great resignation phenomenon. However, the pace of change is increasing, and her book is THE field manual on navigating the turbulent social psychological waters. Although she and I perhaps use slightly different terms to center the need for 'safety and health' concerns, our messages are the same. I wholeheartedly endorse her message that systemic thinking, integration of people and technical systems, and trust-based leadership are the critical ingredients to the new arrangement of people in time and space. Wellbeing is the goal and intentionally designing our social networks is the means to becoming 'future ready'. Get this book, read it and meditate upon the wisdom. This one has got to go in your backpack for the journey forward."

Charles E. Grantham *Ph.D., MSH, FAIS, APF*

"When failures in your high-risk operation are intolerable, how will you ensure success? Like many, I've known for years that efforts toward strengthening diversity, equity, inclusion, and belonging were vital to enabling success in our complex operations. Elusive as these pursuits are, in this book, Rosa shares insights and wisdom from a career dedicated to helping organizations meet these human needs. The techniques and tools are certain to help you sustain the ever-changing relationships and conversations that power our success at critical steps and beyond. Thank you Rosa!"

James Marinus, *Co-author of* Critical Steps, *Operations, High Reliability and Resilience Consultant*

"This book does a superb job of highlighting the significant issues and challenges that many industries and businesses are facing today. Rosa Carrillo has done an outstanding job of researching and shedding light on the causes of dysfunction in modern social systems. She deals with many topics that are not well understood and addressed in current organizational management practice – included in this is the evolving nature of change management, leadership and employee engagement. The author masterfully deals with the role and potential of leadership and relationships to address the complex issues at the heart of organizational performance. This book is a highly significant contribution to the literature on developing human potential and has much to offer to practitioners, scholars and organizations by providing expert insights into where changes are needed and where solutions lie. I highly recommend it."

Brett Read, *Co-author of the Amazon best seller*, Safety Performance Reimagined

"This book supplies the missing pieces for a holistic safety program. In particular, the discussions around Psychosocial Hazards (PSH) and the real impact they have on a safety culture were eye opening."

Matthew Coward, *Team Lead, Former Nuclear Power Plant Refueling Outage Manager*

"Rosa Antonia Carrillo has penned a remarkable book. She has taken the often-misunderstood concepts of Psychological Safety, Engagement, Diversity and Equity and with data as her guide turned these charged ideas into common sense leadership tools. The book is clear, to the point, and agenda free. In a world characterized by volatility, uncertainty, complexity and ambiguity, *Health and Safety Leadership Strategy* will clear away the clutter and is a must read for anyone serious about leadership."

David J Dunnington, *Executive Coach, CEO, Our Best Work*

Health and Safety Leadership Strategy

How Authentically Inclusive
Leaders Inspire Employees to
Achieve Extraordinary Results

Rosa Antonia Carrillo

Routledge
Taylor & Francis Group

LONDON AND NEW YORK

Designed cover image: Rosa Carrillo

First published 2023
by Routledge
4 Park Square, Milton Park, Abingdon, Oxon OX14 4RN

and by Routledge
605 Third Avenue, New York, NY 10158

Routledge is an imprint of the Taylor & Francis Group, an informa business

British Library Cataloguing-in-Publication Data
A catalogue record for this book is available from the British Library

Library of Congress Cataloging-in-Publication Data
Names: Carrillo, Rosa Antonia, author.
Title: Health and safety leadership strategy: how authentically inclusive leaders inspire employees to achieve extraordinary results? / Rosa Antonia Carrillo.
Description: New York, NY : Routledge, 2023. | Includes bibliographical references and index. | Identifiers: LCCN 2022055845 | ISBN 9781032437583 (hardback) | ISBN 9781032437569 (paperback) | ISBN 9781003368724 (ebook)
Subjects: LCSH: Leadership. | Work environment—Psychological aspects. | Personnel management. | Employee motivation.
Classification: LCC HM1261 .C377 2023 | DDC 303.3/4—dc23/eng/20221117 LC record available at https://lccn.loc.gov/2022055845

ISBN: 9781032437583 (hbk)
ISBN: 9781032437569 (pbk)
ISBN: 9781003368724 (ebk)

DOI: 10.4324/9781003368724

Typeset in Bembo
by codeMantra

Contents

Foreword   xi
Acknowledgments   xiii
Prologue   xv

1 Introduction   1
Definition of terms 2
Overview of chapters 4

2 The authentically inclusive leader   7
Philosophy of inclusivity 8
Relationship as the cornerstone of higher performance 13
Expanding inclusion and belonging beyond "we're the same" 15
Self-inquiry 16

3 The societal shifts redefining the acceptable workplace   19
Toxic culture was the #1 reason for resignations 21
Women, teachers and healthcare workers leaving the workplace 22
Most senior leaders plan to join the great resignation 24
Diversity and inclusion implementation and effectiveness 25
Opportunities for change 29

4 Psychosocial risk and mental health   33
Worldwide 750,000 deaths linked to long hours each year 33
Work-related PSH and risk examples 34
The relationship between management and employees as a PSH 34
Racial, gender and social class discrimination as PSHs 36
Mitigating the psychosocial risk of discrimination 41
The psychosocial risks of the hybrid work environment 42

The mental health during Covid-19 and after 44
Emotional culture of compassion lowers burnout 48

5 The secret life of human social systems   52
*Complexity insights transformed our understanding of social
    human systems 53*
Identity and belonging 55
Social fields 59
Generative social fields 63
What is the relationship between human and technical systems? 64
How do you measure results in the social system? 68
Human social systems view of organizations 71

6 People-centered change management   75
Change is a nonlinear process 75
Conversation as a recurring change mechanism 76
*Using the complexity model a new set of assumptions define modern
    change management 77*
Properties of organizational transformation 80
But wait…you've tried benchmarking and it didn't work! 84
Organizational improvement initiatives are relational processes 87
Learning and change are the same process 88
Questions to assess anxiety and change readiness 93
Implications for human resources 93

7 A critical look at psychological safety   96
Who is responsible for generating PS 97
The risks of candid expression 98
Five core social needs for PS 102
PS doesn't come from on high: it is local 102
Practices for inclusion and PS 103

8 Relationship strategies that improve performance   106
First recognize the risks of social interaction 107
Communication bridges 109
Bridge building strategies 111
Managing and influencing political relationships 114

9 Health and safety—an emergent leadership strategy   117
The daily work life of an H&S advisor 119
Shift to core business identity and status 123
Establishing the H&S leadership role 125

10 Getting to inclusion and belonging   127

It starts with me 128
Applications of identity, belonging and inclusion to leadership 130
Voice: having it, losing it and finding it 131
Changing the world through the power of inclusion 133
Enactment is the final step that leads to personal transformation 135

Appendix A: Authentically inclusive leadership practices   137
Appendix B: The confrontation meeting   139
Appendix C: Rapid relationality process   141
Index   142

Foreword

The book you have in front of you is an invitation. It has always been a mantra of mine to *"Only go where you are invited."* This book invites you to deeply explore your organization's current and desired evolution toward common purpose and shared vision. It invites you into a conscious choice about your next indicated step along the path of your life's work. Every chapter builds logically onto the next. This journey of the chapters is built on many decades of competent, purposeful experience.

Early in the book in Chapter 2, the framework for Authentically inclusive Leadership is highlighted. Centered on relationships, this chapter establishes the foundation for the chapters following. Accountability, as Rosa writes about, will never manifest without inclusion. Authentic trust is now a core leadership competency.

Chapter 3 gives a solid overview of what we have experienced through Covid-19 and the resulting emergence of Diversity and Inclusion. Chapter 4 is an eloquent analysis of the greatest threat to the workplace today—the threat to *mental health.* Comprehensively covering the spectrum from discrimination to classism, psychosocial realities of hybrid work and the benefits of creating a compassionate culture, Chapter 4 is another key element to the book's message.

Chapter 5 provides solid proven models and processes to bring organizational transformation into the field of possibilities to those leaders who have never been exposed to them." Explored at length are Complexity, Belonging, Social Fields, GSF's, Human–Technology integration, Measuring Results and Organizational Social Systems.

Chapter 6 now deepens the transformational journey into analyzing the criticality of relationships. The deliverables of these key elements are the synthesis of learning and change. Effectively they become one as Rosa explains in the effectiveness of leadership commitment to evolving their organization.

Chapter 7 defines the trendy Psychological Safety concept in terms of what it is, and isn't. Building communication "Bridges" is addressed as a critical success factor of effective leadership in the transformational lexicon. Industry expert-based case studies and models are provided with the necessary clarity to anchor the deepening of the work.

Chapter 8 gets to the true heart of effectiveness in clarifying strategies that improve performance. This chapter illuminates how information, the lifeblood of any organization, flows through a channel of deep trust. The individual sense of self, ability to process emotions in a self-referential way and interpersonal conscious collaborations are substantive takeaways in this chapter. Intrinsic motivation and its playing field of internal locus of control are allowed to evolve in this environment. Self-actualization in our relationship to our work is the new frontier birthed from an unhealthy legacy. As pointed out in this chapter all perceptions come through our beliefs formed from our experiences. The unfolding of our humanity is a key deliverable of Chapter 8.

Chapter 9 puts us onto the final approach for the fruits of the book's wisdom. The central role of Health and Safety professionals at all levels is observed, analyzed and positioned for consciously choosing its future. Its ROI now moves to its correlation to revenue streams. The weaving of Health and Safety through every organization's DNA will be a non-negotiable attribute to attract current and future talent. Current generations are demanding it; future generations won't consider engagement without it. Any semi-conscious observer knows the growth economy is dying and the sustainable, quality of working life based emergent economy is beginning the difficult and never-ending journey to a higher consciousness and what we know we are called to do.

Chapter 10 puts us squarely in the Yes/No box in the decision tree of moving forward to a more positive future. Accepting what is and committing to what will be is an emergent theme of this final chapter. Reality therapy and conscious choices are Health and Safety leadership's new mandate. Their new mission is to expand the capacity of the organization and optimize its potential. Every leader's scorecard should contain percent of under-utilized potential on it. Allowing any form of leadership moving forward that can't identify, acquire, integrate and optimize talent in an environment of deep Health and Safety must never be considered. Any leader who can't create an environment of Health and Safety at all levels is at best incompetent, at worst criminal. This chapter brings into the open that all leaders need to decide if they can or not commit to organizational Health and Safety.

It is my desire that you see this book as an opening salvo to the end of "control over" to the new liberating environments of "power with" people to transform the workplace into what we all know intuitively it can be. Leadership's desire to control the operating environment rather than embracing collaboration and co-creating will never allow an organization evolve to what could be. Control's end game is compliance, never an energy field that will allow for true Health and Safety. At the subconscious level control is still an internalized parent-child relationship. A leader's ability to allow collaboration and co-creation is the transformational experience of actualization through an adult-to-adult relationship. Let your leadership be a powerful node on the network. A talent integration network. May we all avoid the peril of being badly led.

Terry Musch
Transformational leadership coach

Acknowledgments

A book like this has many authors because it is based on the life experience of so many people who have contributed to making our organizations a better place to work. I am especially grateful to Terry Musch whom I spoke to almost every day to keep me going. He also wrote my foreword while struggling with substantial health issues. He is a coach of the first order, found somewhat of a shaman, someone who can help you find strengths and talents you did not know were there.

My readers and critics, Ron Gantt and Gary Wong helped me to stay on track and called me on my assumptions. James Marinus holds a special place in my heart because he generously contributed to my understanding of interdisciplinary conversations. His work is outstanding and he is very humble. Andy Barker introduced me to James Cameron who made my book richer with his knowledge of technology and its connection to human performance. Drew Rae was essential to helping me articulate the safety and health advisors identity. And John Green is brilliant at articulating those paradoxes that we all struggle with and helping us through them.

As always, I could turn to my mother for inspiration when I felt like quitting. She has never quit anything in her life. My close friends stood by me even though I spent most of my time glued to my computer. I was afraid I would look up and find myself alone. Instead they are there for me.

I have written the names of people who made their comments public on LinkedIn so that others might recognize that there is an army of people all over the world working for dignity, respect and equity in the workplace. I am very proud to be a part of such a community. They are the unseen guardians of safety and health, risk management and mental health whom most people are never aware of.

Of course I cannot end my acknowledgments without making special note of what Edgar Schein has contributed to my work. Though sadly he passed in 2023, I will always consider him a mentor and inspiration. You will see him noted as a reference throughout, but what you cannot see is the generosity of his spirit in supporting and developing upcoming generations.

Prologue

My colleague and I were conversing about this book and I asked him what motivated him to be so generous with his time in supporting the writing of this book. He said, "My mother taught me to always be kind to others." In that moment I felt a sense of peace and my stress over whether this book would be good enough was gone. When I shared my feeling of peace and lightness, our third colleague said, "I felt exactly the same way!" It seems that the word *kind* has magical properties when spoken in sincerity.

Some of us did not get the opportunity to experience the kindness lesson at home. We had to learn it on our own or perhaps still haven't. It's never too late. We can begin by being kind to ourselves. That is how we begin to feel kindness toward others. And that leads to creating a space where people feel included, that they belong. This book shows how simple it is to be inclusive and authentic once we have made the decision to be kinder to ourselves and others. I'm not asking you to believe me. I'm asking you to search inside yourself and find the part of you that knows it.

As of the writing of this book, it is 30 years after the central South LA race riots. The Los Angeles Times did a retrospective and sadly nothing has changed in that neighborhood in spite of all the political promises. Businesses never opened there, even grocery stores are scarce.

In the same year as the riots, 1992, Gloria Steinem wrote *Revolution from Within*. She tells a story of a group of Black high school students who joined a chess club and suddenly began excelling scholastically. Everyone thought it was the chess program so all the schools wanted one. When Gloria interviewed the club members she asked them what they had been doing before Bill Hall, the chess teacher, had arrived. They said things like "hanging out in the street and feeling like shit." Then she asked if there was anything in their school books that helped them improve their grades. "No, not until Mr. Hall thought we were smart, and then we were."

"He thought we were smart." Let that sink in. We do not know we are smart until we are in the presence of someone who thinks we are and treats us that way. George H. Mead (1934),[1] famous sociologist, said we only know we exist as individuals because we interact with other people. I hope the point is not lost that it wasn't learning to play chess that made them smarter, it was the reason they could learn to play that is the lesson here.

The seemingly magical effect of our expectations on how well others learn and work is well documented (Rosenthal & Jacobson, 1968).[2,3] But this goes deeper than one person's expectations or beliefs about the capabilities of another human being. We must also provide a context for knowledge. People who do not have access to the context are left behind. It's teachers like Bill Hall who provide that context by letting young people know that they do belong in the classroom because they have the ability to learn. Individuals who work in the helping professions, mostly unknowingly, communicate "you matter" to employees.

No one is excluded from the benefits of this recovery due to their lack of talent or willingness. If anyone feels that way, our society has failed them. In *Transforming Knowledge*, Elizabeth Kamarck wrote that the root cause of failure in our educational programs in the ghetto was the same problem in universities.

> The root problem appears in all fields and throughout the dominant tradition. It is, simply, that while the majority of humankind was excluded from the making of what has been called knowledge, the dominant few not only defined themselves as the included kind of human but also as the norm in the ideal.
>
> A few privileged men defined themselves as constituting mankind. Then they created root definitions of what it means to be human that, with the concepts and theories that flowed from and reinforce those definitions, made it difficult to think well about, or about the motive, of anyone other than themselves, just as they made it difficult to think honestly about the defining few.
>
> (p. 102)[4]

People in the minority often feel like they can't disagree with people of higher power. They have to be silent and take self-protective measures. A Black woman explains, "I control myself because I want to keep my job." Another says, "I'm able to keep my cool because people have been telling me shut up all my life." A nurse says, "I know how to survive with crazy people screaming at me. I've experienced disrespect for the so long that this is just one more."

Black men say they learn to absorb body blows. Their role model is Mohammed Ali who took a lot of punches and just shook them off. They talk about it as being indicative of what happens every day in America. "There are times when I thought I should say something but I didn't because it happens so much." It's not just the USA. In Paris most children from west Africa are Muslims. So M became the N word of France.

I struggle as I write this book. I don't want to be pigeonholed into only writing about safety and health or about discrimination, but it found me and became my area of expertise. Maybe I will be like the Black woman who told me she went to a Black Lives Matter (BLM) protest and suddenly people started looting. One of the looters offered to protect her and escort her to her car. "That was a wake up moment," she said, "Yes I will accept this privilege." Suddenly, what used to be a pigeonhole became an access to a different kind of power.

If you have read this far you are not someone who is afraid of self-examination and talking about race. I am glad to connect with you. It has been lonely with even some of my best friends not understanding why racism and discrimination pushed me into depression and self-doubt. I am grateful for the protests against the killing of George Floyd because it opened up a national, even global conversation about the personal suffering instigated by discrimination against people who are different from the accepted standards of looks, status or how you live your life. When my friend of 30 years said to me, "I finally understand that you experienced pain in a way that I never felt." I cried relieved at the acknowledgment and then I cried again because it had never occurred to me that she should understand.

Perhaps it is time for optimism. Events impel leadership to embrace the total wellbeing of employees—psychological, physical and mental. Among these responsibilities is an issue that needs urgent attention—the psychological wellbeing of our leaders, H&S personnel, nurses, teachers, caregivers and other important helping professions. The work has begun. Hopefully my book will add to the momentum.

Notes

1 Mead, G. H. (1934). *Mind, self and society.* Chicago University Press: Chicago, IL.
2 Rosenthal, R., & Jacobson, L. (September 1968). Pygmalion in the classroom. *The Urban Review, 3(1), 16–20.*
3 Rosenthal, R., & Jacobson, L. (1992). *Pygmalion in the classroom: Teacher expectation and pupils' intellectual development (Newly expanded ed.).* Crown House Publishing: Bancyfelin, Carmarthen, Wales.
4 Kamarck, E. (2005). *Transforming knowledge* (2nd ed., p. 102). University Press: Philadelphia, PA.

1   Introduction

- The impact and emerging outcomes of Covid-19
- Definition of terms
- Overview of chapters

The confluence of Covid-19, the resulting burnout, the attention on diversity, equity and inclusion generated by the social justice movements and the Great Resignation created an opening to radically improve the employer-employee relationship. This book describes the opportunities and challenges employers face in retaining talent and remaining strategically competitive with both quantitative and qualitative data. The concepts and solutions offered lie in discovering and fully developing people's potential.

Covid-19 broke through the remaining barriers to international connectivity. My social and business life will be defined as pre and post Covid as will the lives of many others of all ages. School children now have friends all over the world and I have new colleagues from Norway to Brazil, Australia and the UK. I just met a virtual connection from Mexico in person and we embraced as long-time friends.

Our global connectedness became more visible. The pandemic demonstrated dependency on each other for our health. If one part of the population does not have adequate healthcare the illness begins there and exposes the rest of the population. It is an awakened awareness that we are all connected.

The Black Lives Matter (BLM) movement struck a global pain point. According to a Wikipedia article (2020) protests took place in over 60 countries and on all seven continents. The protests took place during the Covid-19 pandemic. Gathering in crowds was strongly advised against in some parts of the world, and was illegal in others. In countries like Denmark and Finland people gathered by the thousands. I was most moved by the small numbers that protested in countries like Kazakhstan and Kampala, and Uganda where the potential penalties were severe.

Many question the long-term impact of the protests indicating that very little has changed. There is also backlash from those who felt that the movement's message was that only Black Lives Matter.

DOI: 10.4324/9781003368724-1

Little has changed structurally. Hiring diversity officers does not create leadership if that person has no authority and lacks access to power. We have a long way to go to operationalize gender and racial inclusion and equity. It is a daunting task to change the corporate culture and power structure. Nevertheless, I have seen a greater openness globally to speak of discrimination and exclusion in business organizations.

The Great Resignation somewhat leveled the playing field between employer and employee because there was a shortage of staff in almost every type of business. People took the opportunity to claim their right to have greater control in their personal life. They left toxic work environments and long hours in favor of personal wellbeing and spending more time with family.

Many corporations published their position on inclusion and diversity because of market pressures. The reality of changing global demographics is making it necessary to accept and work with diversity. Research from the London School of Economics (2018) indicates that for countries like the United States and Canada, racial and ethnic minorities will make up the majority of the population somewhere toward 2050. In western Europe it will happen around the end of this century. We need to be mindful of what this means for our diversity and inclusion strategies.

In spite of this awakening the research will show that diversity has made little progress especially in the senior ranks. Yet, the established hierarchy is still threatened and will not go silently. Policies to protect people from bullying or harassment can be seen as a threat to silence the rights of those accustomed to saying whatever they want without consequences. Those who support diversity and inclusion initiatives would do well to take into account the potential backlash against well intentioned DEI initiatives.

This book does not attempt to provide an implementation guide. It is primarily focused on the leader's influence on psychological transformation.

Unconscious bias is the new challenge to bringing our entire organizations along. We may not know that it is a bias making us think that someone isn't right for the job. We can tell ourselves all kinds of stories that make sense to us about why someone doesn't fit in. But until we do the hard work of becoming self-aware and risk having open conversations about our doubts, it will be hard to progress.

People all over the world participated in the BLM movement. The importance of relationships and our interdependence was highlighted by the Covid-19 pandemic. This is the time to make diversity and inclusion more than an initiative to contract with minority vendors. The task will call for authentically inclusive leadership.

Definition of terms

Diversity, equity, inclusion and belonging (DEIB)

Workplace diversity is the range of human differences present within a company, including but not limited to race, ethnicity, gender identity, sexual orientation, age, and social class. Inclusion is the act of making a person part of a group, where each member is afforded the same rights and opportunities.

(Culture amp, 2019: 2)

It has a direct impact on whether people feel a sense of belonging, feel heard and feel safe to express themselves authentically.

According to reports the companies progressing at the greatest pace are those where *inclusion* is not a separate initiative. It is integrated into the way work is done. I was asked during a safety conference panel if there's a difference between psychological safety (PS) and DEIB. I and the other panelists agreed that there is no difference in terms of safety performance. I would wager that applies to all types of operational performance. People cannot perform at their best if these needs are not met (Culture amp, 2019).[1]

Authentically inclusive leadership

Adding *authentically* before *inclusive leadership* was done with great thought. Too many times we use the term *employee engagement* or *inclusive leadership* and find that employees have become skeptical of them. It is same with the use of *empowerment*. Most often these terms did not lead to improvements in the employee experience.

There are five main descriptors for inclusive leadership as defined by informal surveys and discussions. They are self-awareness, emotional maturity, intentionality, ethical behavior and fluid mindset. These are not the only characteristics but they are essential to one's ability to let go of bias and see the world from the perspective of other people's experiences.

Psychological safety

Edgar Schein and Warren Bennis (1965) wrote that anxiety must be reduced for learning and personal change to take place. They called it a sense of psychological safety.

Amy Edmondson makes it clear that she is talking about improving organizational performance psychological safety, as opposed to personal growth.

> Psychological safety is defined as a belief that speaking up with ideas, questions, concerns, or mistakes is expected and feasible, and is best summarized as a sense of permission for candor. Yet despite awareness of the concept, misunderstanding remains – inhibiting many from undertaking the serious effort needed to make conversations work as they should. For instance, some executives worry privately that creating psychological safety will result in too much cross-talk or unleash endless chatter, gobbling up valuable time, slowing progress, or creating confusion. Or worse, people might speak up in unproductive ways – complaining endlessly or expecting someone else to fix the problems they raise. People intuitively understand that all voice is not productive – and that some silence is indeed golden.

This makes it hard for them to know how to balance soliciting input with maintaining efficiency. As a result, they err on the side of efficiency.

Amy Edmondson

Throughout this book *PS* is used interchangeably with the states it creates such as *inclusion and belonging* and *equity and inclusion, respect, security and autonomy*. I do so because the term PS has become overused and oversimplified. If people don't feel included or respected they do not feel psychologically safe.

Human social systems

Social systems are sometimes referred to as human systems. I use the term human social systems to highlight the impact of social influences on group formation and individuals. The word system can be misleading because systems thinking theory implies an orderly arrangement and intra-relationship of parts where every part plays a definite role. However, the human system is characterized by emergence and nonlinearity. An example is that there are consistent social needs that most people require for wellbeing, learning and creativity. One could assume that the absence of having these needs met would automatically result in poor development. Nevertheless, marginalized individuals living in deprivation manage to creatively solve problems that others cannot.

Generative social fields

Generative social fields (GSFs) per Böll (2018) describe the social conditions that engender learning, belonging, self-esteem and self-actualization. They are safe spaces where two or more gather to learn or solve systemic problems. The middle school where I mentor is working on environmental control for their neighborhood.

Individuals feel safe to fail, learn from failure and be themselves. Senge et al. (2015) developed this concept working with students from primary schools and universities.

Overview of chapters

The principles and methods in this book are currently in use by leaders to create commitment, accountability and excellence. Each chapter covers the information managers and leaders need to understand the issues today that impact every aspect of safety, health and organizational performance. Some of those include mental health, the retention of top talent, inclusion of diverse talent and adapting to the hybrid workplace.

These are presented under four themes.

1 **Leader's beliefs about human nature:**
   The first is an introduction to four of the Relationship Centered Leadership Beliefs. These beliefs come from my 30 years of experience working

with leaders who developed high performance teams and organizations. A leader's beliefs about human nature informs their ability to inspire, motivate and bring out the full potential of their direct reports. They serve to engage people in the mental, physical and economic post Covid-19 recovery.

2 **Current state of organizational mental, physical and psychological wellbeing:**
The second theme is the current state of wellbeing in our organizations that point to the need for immediate action. Employers must pay attention to the data to keep their top talent and essential workers. Chapters 2 and 3 consist of current research on the social, psychological and critical business issues that impact organizational recovery from the Covid-19 and burnout pandemic. Interviews with safety and health advisors that carried the brunt of the pandemic response at work reveal the sometimes overwhelming challenges that led to the Great Resignation. Organizations are faced with preventing and mitigating psychosocial hazards and injuries which have become more frequent than physical injuries. These conditions make the mental health and wellbeing of employees a priority for business and government leaders.

3 **Human social systems basics for managers:**
The third theme covers social systems thinking and its impact on change management and leadership development. The challenges presented by the data will not be resolved by technology or traditional change management practices. Chapters 4–6 are a basic primer of how social systems and psychological safety impact operations. These are concepts not covered in traditional business school curriculum and are essential to adequately addressing psychosocial hazards and injuries, which now outnumber reported physical injuries in the workplace. They also cover the socio psychological challenges and risks involved in change management. Rather than present a step-by-step framework, this book gets into the small iterative actions that build the relationship between leader and follower, then between team members. These are the important conversations that form the norms and assumptions that drive human performance.

4 **Response strategies that address social human systems**
Finally, the fourth theme is a set of response strategies to repair and improve relationships, trust and communication. The solutions fall under the human social systems and offer people the opportunity to utilize their full potential. Chapters 7 and 8 contain practical everyday leadership actions that build workplaces where it is safe to learn, fail, innovate and speak your mind for the benefit of the organization. These principles, concepts and actions arm leaders with the tools they need to succeed in this new business environment. This would include talent

retention, increasing diversity and inclusion as well as improving collaboration across disciplines and breakdown of we/they barriers.

Chapter 9 describes health and safety as a strategy for organizational improvement. The Covid crisis taught us some hard truths. Perhaps foremost was that safety must be a precondition, not something we prioritize. The pandemic was predictable. Yet, we were not ready for it. We lost people at work and at home. Our government and political leaders did not protect the public.

I worked in one company whose employees felt deserted by management. In another, employees lauded management's support during Covid-19. Did that matter? The former had a 33% absenteeism rate and the latter had a rate of 2.5%. The indicators are there. Caring for the wellbeing of employees—the purpose of the health and safety function—raises up the entire organization. So why not leverage that power consciously?

Chapter 10 looks at the leadership journey from bias to inclusion; and from fitting in to authenticity. Only with a constancy of focus can the people of an organization believe it's really true that management cares about them. Only then will the training and problem solving and improvement capabilities take hold in normal times and especially under stress.

Note

1 Culture amp's (2019) survey analyzed responses from 5,100 companies and 34M respondents.

Bibliography

Böll, M. M. (2018). Introduction to the meeting. In Brochure for the first gathering in generative social fields, October 1–3, 2018. Garrison, NY.

Culture amp. (2019). 2019 Diversity and inclusion report. Accessed July 23, 2022. https://cdn2.hubspot.net/hubfs/516278/2019_Diversity_and_Inclusion.pdf

Edmondson, A. C., & Besieux, T. (2021). Reflections: Voice and silence in workplace conversations. *Journal of Change Management, 21*(3), 269–286. Accessed May 6, 2021. https://www.tandfonline.com/doi/full/10.1080/14697017.2021.1928910?scroll=top&needAccess=true

List of George Floyd protest outside of the United States. Accessed July 14, 2022. https://en.wikipedia.org/wiki/List_of_George_Floyd_protests_outside_the_United_States#Antarctica

London School of Economics. (2018). Rising ethnic diversity in the West may fuel a (temporary) populist right backlash. Accessed July 23, 2022. https://blogs.lse.ac.uk/politicsandpolicy/ethnic-diversity-transitions-effect/

Schein, E. H., & Bennis, W. G. (1965). *Personal and organizational change through group methods: The laboratory approach.* United Kingdom: Wiley.

Senge, P., Scharmer, O., & B.ll, M. (2015). Towards a lexicon for investigating generative social fields. A report prepared for the Mind-Life Institute Academy for Contemplative and Ethical Leadership.

2   The authentically inclusive leader

- Relationship-centered leadership
- Defining inclusion within accountability
- Self-inquiry as a catalyst for authenticity

Authenticity is something leaders do rather than a character trait. Being seen as authentic means that your words and actions align. It means that people perceive that how you express yourself reflects how you feel inside. Thus an authentic act of inclusion communicates respect and recognition.

Inclusion and authenticity expand the traditional leadership capabilities. Becoming adept at inclusion will increase a leader's ability to navigate through the present crisis and into creating the future of work. But people are quick to pick up inauthentic behavior. Inclusiveness and authenticity cannot be faked for long.

Of course, being authentic is easier if you were already included as a member of the tribe. If you look, walk or talk like others in leadership in your organization, authenticity usually comes easier for you. If that isn't you being authentic and practicing honesty must be accompanied by political savvy or good judgment.

Organizations with authentically inclusive leaders are more likely to have engaged, enthusiastic, motivated employees and psychologically safe cultures. That is why the topics of social identity, psychological safety (PS) and social fields are covered in depth. Leaders knowledgeable in these areas are better able to bring their full selves to work and encourage employees to do the same.

It is not the intent of this book to argue for what has become known as authentic leadership. It has been proposed that authentic leadership is not gender-neutral and is especially challenging for women because as *outsiders* they are less likely to be accepted by their followers as authentic leaders. It has also been connected to stewardship and spirituality (servant leadership), transformational leadership and ethical leadership (Önday 2016).

In today's society all leaders have to work with multiple cultures. Not just ethnic but also the occupational subcultures in an organization. These groups tend to have low trust and communication with each other when they

DOI: 10.4324/9781003368724-2

exclude others not like them. It leads to not sharing information in a timely manner and can lead to multiple types of failures. So, it is important for leaders to facilitate communication between subgroups and create opportunities to build trust.

But, culture can pose obstacles to including those who are different because its purpose is to provide security and stability by clarifying what behavior is allowed and who is part of the tribe. A country, religion or ethnic group's culture provides the answer to those questions. You can find them identified in Hofstede's work on culture (2022).

Covid-19 and the Black Lives Matter movement opened an opportunity to make inclusivity a reality. The shared struggle connected us. People were crying together; many spoke about realizing just how important their relationships were in their life. Bob Kunz, Corporate Safety Director, shared:

> I am reflecting upon Covid-19 and the workplace. Is the "shared experience" the legacy of Covid-19? And, If it is, how do we create and maintain the shared experience during everyday ordinary work?

Indeed, we are pretty good at tapping into our connectivity during crisis. I believe we can consciously choose to evolve a more constant awareness of our connection to each other. It may be required for survival as our planet becomes more populated and technology increases our capacity for destruction.

Philosophy of inclusivity

Neuroscience discovered we have a need to belong or be included is as important to our survival as food and shelter. That is a very sobering thought. First because there are millions of people who do not experience inclusion and second because we have to reflect on what we would do for food if we were starving. The science indicates that lacking a sense of belonging can drive people to desperate actions. And, we have seen that manifested in the United States with young men who feel ostracized shooting children in schools.

Human nature with its need to belong is not any different than the other forms of nature that surround us. You cannot threaten or motivate a tree to grow taller. You can water it, fertilize it and make sure it is planted in the right soil with sunny conditions. It is the same with people. Organizations spend a lot of time on management systems. Having the right technology, rewards, training and controls is important. Yet little attention is paid to those things without which people cannot grow or thrive. The right action is to provide people with environments that meet their social needs. Primary among them being inclusion and belonging.

That means that most business leaders will need to set new priorities, which means adopting new beliefs about people. In my work with leaders over the past 30 years I collected eight beliefs about human nature that led to successfully engaging employees in high-performance organizations. The first four relate to inclusion and belonging in the workplace (Carrillo, 2020).

1 Inclusion precedes accountability.
2 True communication takes place in the presence of relationship and trust.
3 Innovation, resilience, inclusion and accountability are interdependent.
4 People are able and willing to contribute to the success of the enterprise.

These beliefs are at the core of what this book proposes to operationalize as part of the strategy for recovery from Covid-19 and stepping into the challenges before us now—new jobs that challenge and pay well, climate change, mental health, clean water, homelessness and so much more. For those who do not already hold these beliefs, internalizing them may require letting go of some long-standing negative experiences. That takes self-inquiry and a willingness to change.

Inclusion precedes accountability

What is inclusion? What does it have to do with accountability?

Inclusion is an act that allows another being into your circle of relationship. It engenders a sense of belonging that raises one's sense of security and of being valued by others. It brings a sense of being seen and heard—a temporary melding of you and I into we. In that state human beings have greater access to their creativity, compassion, ability to share and acceptance of others. They become engaged and a source of tremendous wisdom.

Inclusion is a powerful motivator because the need to belong is as strong as the need for food, shelter and physical safety. When a leader creates a field of inclusion, people are motivated to engage. Fear of exclusion or ostracism is unconsciously connected to fear of physical harm or death. This is why lack of inclusion lowers accountability, performance and wellbeing.

Inclusiveness drives out fear, exclusion creates silence and withdrawal. There is no accountability in a fear-driven organization where people feel they don't matter—that they are peripheral to the important work that needs to get done. Why would anyone be motivated to take on responsibility, go beyond minimum requirements, or contribute their creativity if he or she didn't feel they were an important part of the solution? And, how do people know they are important at work? They know when they are included in decision-making; when their opinions are sought out and their work respected. They know it when they feel they belong in a trusted circle. These are the proof of inclusion.

Accountability is a loaded word. There are many that say blame stops learning and communication. The last conversation I facilitated about ending blame and transforming accident investigations into learning opportunities came to a halt with this question, "How will we hold people accountable?"

There are corporate liabilities that must be balanced with employee perceptions of fairness. Leaders know that using disciplinary measures to hold people accountable can shut down communication. On the other hand, not holding people accountable can spark accusations of favoritism and unfairness.

Self-accountability is sought after for these reasons. But unless it is accompanied by autonomy and empowerment, employees often perceive it as "blame the worker." They feel it is unfair when they don't have power over the systems that lead to most failures. True self-accountability and personal responsibility are the results of strong inner convictions and a culture where their expression is encouraged. Therefore it cannot take place in an environment where people do not feel included and valued.

True communication takes place in the presence of relationship and trust

Trust and inclusion are precursors to achieving organizational excellence. Relationship building is the vehicle to deliver belonging, inclusion and trust. The words relationship building can bring up immediate resistance in the workplace. Many consider it an irrelevant subject that detracts from getting the work done. In fact, a widely recognized study found that out of 60,000 leaders less than 5% excel at both achieving important results and building social relationships (Lieberman, 2013). Only 18% of current managers believe they need to create the relationships with employees to help teams achieve excellence (Gallup, 2015).

The information we need to prevent failure and thrive is all around us, but we may have to go outside our usual channels to get it. It is possible that people may not be speaking up because they feel we are too busy or don't want to hear it. It is possible that at this very moment people are talking amongst themselves about malfunctioning processes that will eventually result in damaging the company's reputation. Such conversations typically take place informally between small numbers of people and are hidden because they go against the politically correct storyline. If the leader doesn't go after it systematically, communicate it to others that need to know and act on it, it will stay hidden.

Organizational trust between employees and managers is recognized as important to performance (Bastug, et al., 2016; Aryee, et al., 2002). Without trust it is almost impossible to get information in a timely and accurate manner. Trust requires some form of relationship. Since each profession tends to communicate within its own boundaries, others may not get information that could impact their work. Breaking down silos is a matter of relationship building across disciplines and functions.

These shortfalls can be serious barriers to enlisting the buy-in needed to shift structures, practices and systems to adapt to shifting conditions. Business managers who idealize "lean" and "just-in-time" operations without understanding that the quality of social relationships in the organization is a critical influence on performance.

Communication is a skill that needs to be learned, and many people grew up in homes where healthy conflict resolution wasn't demonstrated or taught to them. Conflict is sure to surface and knowing how to handle it in a healthy manner can help mitigate damage caused by careless words and even strengthen the bond in the long run.

Companies face a challenge much bigger than increasing share price. It is the challenge of maintaining a quality of life that includes the wellbeing of our planet as well as humanity. I believe that corporate success versus wellbeing is a false dichotomy. We can achieve both if we manage the social side of our organizations as carefully as we manage the financial and technical aspects. Doing that will require adopting a new mindset. It happened before with the end of feudalism, the renaissance and the many declarations of independence from colonization. Now corporations are facing new frontiers. As evidence mounts that diversity and inclusivity are a competitive edge, companies realize that failure to adapt will result in loss of business.

Innovation, resilience and inclusion are interdependent

Inclusion is interdependent with resilience and innovation. Google's team development research (Duhigg, 2016) showed how inclusion and PS shows up as innovation. They found that the #1 characteristic of their high-performance teams was that they were absent of ridicule, thus allowing team members to freely express any idea. Even if a far-fetched idea failed the creator was not in danger of ostracism.

Relationships are the foundation of an organization. This reality is reflected in society by the tradition of falling in love, courting, marriage and building a family and community. In an organization it is the partnerships between employer and employee as well as peer-to-peer that are the foundation. A successful partnership is founded on the willingness of the stronger member to hold up the one who may have less power. In so doing they recognize the dignity and value of that person and their contributions. When the leader is aware that in reality they could do nothing without such followers this forms an attraction that leads to trust and commitment. It is far more powerful than simply talking about people as our greatest asset.

Every organization must take some risk to get to innovation, and if we take risks sometimes we fail, so we need resilience to try again. I'm not talking about taking physical risks. I'm talking about psychosocial risk. We don't talk about the risks we most often ask people to take like speaking up about mistakes. We ask them to report near misses. We tell them to ask questions that could reveal that they have less knowledge or expertise than their peers. We ask them to contribute their best ideas even though they might get rejected.

If we ask people to take these risks then we must provide timely support if we expect them to be resilient. Till now we have asked people to bounce back from mergers, acquisitions, layoffs, outsourcing and Covid-19. We see the results of these demands in the level of resignations. In response companies offer more mental health benefits. But what we need to do is create a climate of inclusion. For that purpose we added the concept of micro-inclusive practices for leaders and an appendix with specific recommendations.

Here is a radical suggestion for any leader who wishes to succeed in becoming inclusive. Use the quiet people and those in the minority as sensors for the weak signals that predict loss of trust. Women of color are the most sensitive to those small clues. The reason is that the lower you are on the social hierarchy the more vigilant you have to be to notice the silent signs that people are losing patience or getting upset. This is actually a survival mechanism.

I have a potted plant that I call my "garden canary." It is the first plant to droop for lack of water. That tells me it is time to water the plants. I water it and almost instantly it bounces back. If I were to let the rose bushes get to the point of drooping they would not recover so easily. So it is good to have an early warning of what is about to happen in the garden so I can take preventative action. This works well if you check the garden regularly. Who are the canaries in your family, in your workplace? Who do you watch to keep informed of the emotional state in your organization?

People are able and willing to contribute to the success of the enterprise

Put simply, if you do not believe that people are able and willing to contribute to the success of the enterprise you are not able to access a huge fountain of information. Data to help us avoid the next failure is raining down upon us but we cannot see it or hear it because we aren't listening. And we are not listening because we do not trust the source—our people.

There is so much unfulfilled human potential in this world. The work conditions in many parts of the world are not designed to treat people as the valuable resource they are. When we hear of people like Viktor Frankl rising from the horribly deprived circumstances of a concentration camp to become an important contributor to society, it awakens hope that our external circumstances do not determine who we are.

Leaders have the opportunity to develop people's potential. People perform in response to our expectations of them. They sense our expectations by the way we treat them and the way we treat them is based on our beliefs about them. Responding to expectations is a law of human nature. It applies in classrooms, labs and it certainly applies in the workplace.

It may seem like an exaggeration to say that the first area to look at if you would like to improve performance is your beliefs about what people are willing and capable of contributing. When I was in training to be a teacher I learned about experiments where teachers were told that a random group of children had a genius IQ. The overall performance of those children tended to be higher than the children who the teachers were told were average. All the children were exposed to the same lessons and materials. The only difference was the teacher's belief about their ability to learn. I learned that we unconsciously treat people differently based on what we believe to be true about their capabilities (Rosenthal, 1963; *Rosenthal & Jacobson, 1992*).

Enacting a higher level of performance takes a new set of assumptions and beliefs to interpret the conditions, intentions and events around us. The questions we ask, the influences we investigate and the solutions we consider are directed by the assumption that accountability and results come as a consequence of inclusiveness, respect and valuing of differences. This is a challenge that leaders will certainly be facing as they work to integrate diversity, inclusion and belonging into the way that work is done. The first level of work is always on yourself because many of our biases are unconscious.

Relationship as the cornerstone of higher performance

Relationship is a physical (neurological) and psychological need for human survival. The connections established with others make life meaningful, and influence our physical wellbeing.

There is little written on how work relationships are formed (DiBenigno, 2020). In this book I suggest that *complex responsive processes* explain how the small social interactions between people form the relationship. The actions entail saying thank you, good morning, looking someone in the eyes, learning people's names, being helpful by providing resources or information. These small acts fulfill people's need for inclusion and belonging along with the other needs identified for PS. Among them are the need for autonomy, respect, security and equity.

Relational coordination highlights that effective working relationships are characterized by frequent communication, mutual respect, and shared knowledge and goals (Gittell et al., 2006). But they have not yet identified the micro-processes underlying the creation of these relationships. What this book suggests is that it is the quality of small frequent interactions between people that builds those relationships. Those connections form a common experience of feelings, ways of thinking and working within a group(s).

In *The Relationship Factor in Safety Leadership (2020)* I focused on the neuro and social science to explain why building relationships is one of the most important leadership competencies. I also provided many specific practices and case studies to demonstrate how those relationships are built and the benefits to organizational performance.

This book builds on those ideas to further understand why relationships are the venue through which leaders bring about change in organizations. In a typical framework the leaders' critical role in change management is described as:

- Organizational improvement and culture change are leadership issues
- There is a natural flow to organizational improvement that begins with the leadership team and cascades through the organization
- Employees watch, and model behavior exhibited by the leadership team
- Leadership provides the resources and creates the organizational context
- Leadership creates the aspirational vision of a future state and sets the stage for improvement
- Leadership determines performance metrics
- During change, how leadership responds to failures, successes, setbacks and new ideas really matters
- Leadership can diminish resistance to change

These are valid observations based on years of experience. What is lacking is the context that makes these activities transformative. Science revealed that many of the processes that make things happen in this universe are invisible. Human relations are one of the most opaque processes as will be covered throughout the book.

It is not about friendship: it's a relational partnership

It bears repeating that building relationships to support organizational change is not about friendships or revealing parts of your life that you would rather keep private. Those things are not essential to building working relationships based on trust and accountability. The three most important things in personal relationships are:

1 **Connectedness**. This relational building block can be thought of as connection between people that encourages trust and commitment, and nurtures a sense of acceptance or shared values.
2 **Commitment** can be thought of as a mindful and consistent decision to invest into a relationship by showing up, keeping your word and making decisions that benefit others as well as you. It is this building block that helps push relationships through times of difficulty.
3 **Open communication** allows for a closer connection as well as sharing of work information. The more you are comfortable revealing with a co-worker the more effectively you can work together.

It is a fact that humans respond to relationships (including employer–employee relationships) that satisfy their social need for belonging. Therefore, the satisfaction of that need is the entryway to trust and commitment. Therefore, these three factors also apply to employer–employee relationships.

Relationship building is about investing in your employees to form long-lasting connections that go beyond them doing their job. Through relationship you build a bond with employees that makes them passionate about the company's mission, each other and the product or service you sell.

Relational partnerships generate *commitment and trust*. They are created by stability and reliability as well as a high-quality relating experience. The latter would mean that both parties gain a sense of belonging, personal growth, PS or meaning from their interactions. The nature of these relationships creates generative spaces to work. This is the space where innovation, resilience, inclusion, accountability and wellbeing thrive.

Schein and Schein (2018) bring attention to an important aspect of what I am calling *relational partnerships*. They are personal. In *Humble Leadership* they write that mutual trust grows by getting to know followers on a personal level. Leaders are willing to reveal personal information about themselves and get to know other members of the team in the same way. As a result an equitable relationship emerges where followers are willing to assume responsibility for outcomes and pursue their personal growth.

Case study: It may sound impossible that the success of a change initiative can be stalled by little interactions that may appear to be insignificant at first. An example is an American leader walking past his staff without saying good morning and closing the door to their office. Eventually they were fired because the process changes they were tasked with did not get implemented. It turns out the staff did not follow through because they thought the boss was a rude uncaring person.

One of the staff said to me, "That's not the way we treat each other in the Netherlands. I tried to tell him." A leader's interactions and conversations are carefully observed. Employee engagement, which is critical to the success of change initiatives, rises and falls on the level of trust in the relationship between leader and follower.

Expanding inclusion and belonging beyond *"we're the same"*

PS, inclusion and belonging cannot be mandated. If they are not already part of the culture it takes a transformational process to make it the way members treat each other and a factor in all decisions that affect people. The following map (Figure 1) illustrates the elements that could drive such a transformation and the best possible outcomes. 1. It is usually initiated by a leader who is inclusive and understands the strategic importance of a diverse workforce and creating safe places to learn and fail. Such a leader is self-aware, empathetic and has an inner state of PS.

2. Through those characteristics and actions they develop a *Generative Social Field* where PS dominates in the leadership team. 3. As the field spreads to their direct reports it begins to show up in improved team performance. 4. As more team leaders and teams become high performance, it becomes an organizational phenomenon. The cloud at the end of the process represents

Inclusion and Belonging

(Transformational Process)

Figure 1 Transforming into inclusion and belonging.

the output as a community characterized by self-efficacy, hope, resilience, optimism and purpose.

Chapter 5, *The secret life of human social systems*, explains more on how *Generative Social Fields* work. Chapter 7, *A critical look at PS*, provides more detail into this transformational process. High performance requires many other resources besides PS. Inclusion and belonging is only one critical factor.

Managing the transformation to inclusion and belonging at the team level:

- Generate PS and inclusion as a team norm
- Articulate and keep the shared goal present and clear
- Acknowledge when you don't know the answer or made a mistake
- Structured learning process where reflection follows action
- Use direct actionable language to elicit information and participation from marginalized members
- Set performance goals collaboratively

Self-inquiry

The Self is the true center of your experience in its totality according to Carl Jung. Consequently it is your connection to wisdom—the ability to take action with the whole in mind.

Things are seldom black-and-white when working with human beings. It's even trickier when you are working with multiple cultures because you don't have an inside track on how people are interpreting reality. Taking a position of inquiry opens up to a diversity of information. It also enables alternative solutions that are beyond the usual reactive mode.

This is an opportunity to reflect on your personal beliefs about human nature and how your expectations are affecting the people around you. Everyone affects the people around them by what they say but more power means you have more impact. Even if you do not think of yourself in this way, when you have the title of team leader, supervisor or director, people assign meanings to your words that you may not be aware of. An example is telling someone they are doing a good job in front of another person. The other person may assume you do not believe they are doing a good job unless you specifically address them as well. Unless that person were to tell you how they felt, you would have no way of knowing if you damaged that relationship.

Self-inquiry questions to prepare for reading this book

It would be very arrogant for me to say that reading this book could change the way you approach people-related endeavors hence forward. As you read you may feel the need for scientific evidence that the way people treat each other influences outcomes. There is actually scientific evidence presented later in this book that may convince you. However, consider that Talcott Parsons (1991), one of the most influential sociologists, commented that there are no scientific laws that can provide empirical evidence to explain a change in mental state. But, we can describe the beginning and end states of the process such as changing a relationship from distrust to trust. Or changing an individual's sense of self from excluded to belonging.

The following questions may help you prepare for reading this book by helping you ascertain your state of mind and where you want to go.

- How is my mental health? Am I taking care of myself physically and psychologically?
- What do I believe about good communication practices? How have they served me?
- Do I believe that trust and relationship are necessary for good communication? Do I believe a conversation is the only way of ensuring true communication?
- How do I consciously help people feel that they are included and that they belong? Do I believe that this is important and affects people's ability to perform?
- How do I approach people who I feel have not held themselves accountable? Am I conscious of whether or not that person and I have a relationship of trust and open communication? If not how would I find out?
- What are my beliefs about human nature that impact my relationships with people at work? Do I believe that everyone is willing to contribute according to their abilities?

- Do I believe I need to have some measure of control and oversight? How has that worked for me? How much control do I need?
- Who do I consider part of my social network? Who should I add or let go?
- What are some small steps I can take to improve my relationships and support people in developing their full potential?
- How can I balance the external demands on my time with allocating time for what I feel is important like relationship building?
- How is my state of PS and my sense of belonging? Do I need to take action to improve them?

Bibliography

Aryee, S. Budhwar, P. S., Chen, Z. X. (2002). Trust as a mediator of the relationship between organizational justice and work outcomes: test of a social exchange model. Wiley online library. https://onlinelibrary.wiley.com/doi/abs/10.1002/job.138

Anjum, Z. (2021). Hybrid work is the next big disruption. Accessed July 14, 2022. https://www.linkedin.com/pulse/hybrid-work-next-big-disruption-zubair-anjum/

Bustag, G., Pala, A., Kumartasli, M. Gunel, I. Duyan, M. (2016). Investigation of the relationship between organizational trust and organizational commitment. *Universal journal of education research, 4*(6), 1418–1425.

Carrillo, R. A. (2020). *The relationship factor in safety leadership: Achieving success through employee engagement.* Routledge: London

Catalyst. (2021). The great work life divide. Accessed August 12, 2022. https://www.catalyst.org/research/flexibility-demand-future-of-work/

DiBenigno, J. (2020). Rapid relationality: How peripheral experts build a foundation for influence with line managers. *Administrative Science Quarterly, 65*(1), 20–60.

Duhigg, C. (2016). What Google learned from its quest to build the perfect team. *NY Times.* Downloaded August 29, 2018. https://www.nytimes.com/2016/02/28/magazine/what-google-learned-from-its-quest-to-build-the-perfect-team.html

Gallup. (2015). State of the American Manager, Gallup, April 2015.

Gittell, J.H., Cameron, K., Lim, S., & Rivas, V. (2006). Relationships, layoffs and organizational resilience: The airline industry responses to September 11. *Journal of Applied Behavioral Sciences. 42*(3), 300–329.

Hofstede. (2022). Compare countries. https://www.hofstede-insights.com/fi/product/compare-countries/

Lieberman, M. D. (2013). *Social: Why our brains are wired to connect.* Random House: New York.

Önday, Özgür. (2016). What is the relationship between gender and authentic leadership: Does gender really matter? *Elixir Org. Behaviour, 91,* 38020–38031. https://www.researchgate.net/publication/304352402_What_is_the_Relationship_between_the_Gender_and_Authentic_Leadership_Does_Gender_Really_Matter

Parsons, T. (1991). *Social system.* Routledge: London (p. 138).

Rosenthal, R. (1963). https://www.npr.org/sections/health-shots/2018/09/07/644530036/watch-can-you-affect-another-persons-behavior-with-your-thoughts

Rosenthal, R., & Jacobson, L. (1992). *Pygmalion in the classroom: Teacher expectation and pupils' intellectual development (Newly expanded ed.).* Crown House Publishing: Bancyfelin, Carmarthen, Wales.

Schein, E. H., & Schein, P. (2018). *Humble leadership: The power of relationships.* Berett-Koehler: Oakland, CA.

3   The societal shifts redefining the acceptable workplace

- How Covid-19 accelerated change in the workplace
- Why women and the helping professions joined the great resignation
- We are endangering the status of the professions that serve as the glue of society
- Dealing with the bias of others and our own

The Covid-19 pandemic brought attention to our cultural and socioeconomic weaknesses in a way that could not be ignored. It was a tale of privilege and suffering. The President of the United States contracted Covid and was flown by private helicopter to a hospital suite where he received medications unavailable to anyone but the wealthiest. One can only guess the millions of dollars spent on his speedy recovery.

Others had to be prioritized as there weren't enough ICU beds for everyone that needed one. In particular there were not enough ventilators or critical care resources for all the patients in danger of dying from respiratory or other organ failures. Healthcare givers were forced into deciding who would live and who would die depending on who was most likely to recover. This led to the question, "Are some patients more important?" (Lavaza & Garasic, 2022). We know the answer to that. They are if they have enough money.

The times brought about the best and worst of times. Some of us got to spend more time with family watching the news safely, working from home. While others were forced to work in jobs exposing them to the virus to support themselves and their families. There were shoutouts of gratitude to healthcare heroes and essential workers. Some healthcare workers were cursed at because they didn't have the resources to help. There were loved ones that died alone because their families could not enter the quarantined hospital rooms. And, there were those in the helping professions worried daily about bringing home the virus but hung in there because it was the right thing to do.

It gave everyone a sense of positive contribution to purpose in a caring social context. I did nothing specifically on mental health in the same way that I do very little specifically on safety. Both are outcomes of the way we treat each other. Bill Stettiner, H&S Advisor noted:

DOI: 10.4324/9781003368724-3

Perhaps if anything good has come out of Covid-19, it is the importance of equity, inclusion and belonging. We have seen how reliant we are on people like cleaners, shopkeepers and food delivery drivers. But most importantly we have experienced the need to connect with each other. I hope we keep the lessons from Covid-19.

As teammates started losing friends and relatives, compassion was important. One of my coworkers lost his wife to suicide, and people in general were under considerable strain from being either essential or non-essential (both groups seemed to feel that they were incorrectly categorized). My Sister and Mother were completely convinced that the world was coming to an end. Various friends and colleagues had differing views, and it seemed that very few extremely intelligent people could comprehend any other perspective.

Bill Stettiner, safety & health advisor.

No one faced more stress than healthcare workers. A physician posted the following after a fatality on a movie set in October 2021. The gun was loaded with live ammunition instead of blanks. No one knows how or why.

As a hospital physician who has personally watched many people die unnecessarily of Covid-19, I found the fatal "Rust" filming accident to be a powerful metaphor that might help some people better grasp the pandemic reality that health care workers live with every day. That is, Covid-19 at any gathering of people (work, school, entertainment, etc.) is like having live rounds on a set... People who refuse to vaccinate or follow protocols are live bullets waiting to kill someone.

People who refuse to be vaccinated talked about preserving their freedom. Some claimed to have scientific evidence that the vaccines would have terrible side effects down the line. I had a friend crying telling me that she was being shamed and ostracized for doing what was best for her health. These divisions ended friendships and split up families. All of it added to the constant stress surrounding Covid-19.

But again, there were blessings. One was the proliferation of virtual technology (VT), which changed the workplace and global relations. This would not be the first time that a pandemic would trigger significant social changes. The black plague ended feudalism. It killed millions of people causing a shortage of workers forcing feudal lords to start paying people to tend their lands. But that was not the only reason for humanity's social evolution. The printing press accelerated education and when the Bible became available to everyone, it gave rise to Protestantism and took away the Catholic church's monopoly on Christianity (Weisenthal & Alloway, 2021).

Covid-19 was small compared to the Black Death. But it made formerly invisible essential employees visible such as seafarers so critical to the supply chain and food delivery drivers. VT exploded and played an important role on attitudes about work. The use of VT seems to be leading to a restructuring of the work contract with so many workers wanting to work from home. CNBC and global gender equality firm Catalyst published *The Great Work/ Life Divide (2021)* in which they reported that almost 50% of employees were thinking about quitting their job in the U.S. and 42% of employees said they would quit if their company didn't offer remote working options long term.

Personal values shifted. In October 2021, a global survey found that 65% of women said the pandemic had made them rethink the place that work should have in their life. Fifty-six percent said it made them want to contribute more to society (Wiles, 2022). The change in attitudes contributed to what was coined the "Great Resignation."

> This shift is likely to stick, and it's good for democratizing access to opportunity. Companies in major cities can hire talent from underrepresented groups that may not have the means or desire to move to a big city. And in smaller cities, companies will now have access to talent that may have a different set of skills than they had before.
>
> Karin Kimbrough, Chief Economist at LinkedIn, (Anjum, 2021)

People developed more personal relationships at work. Employees wrote that coworkers leaned on each other in new ways to get through the last year. One in six had cried with a coworker, especially those in healthcare and education (Microsoft work trend index, 2021).

> Before the pandemic, we encouraged people to 'bring their whole self to work,' but it was tough to truly empower them to do that. The shared vulnerability of this time has given us a huge opportunity to bring real authenticity to company culture and transform work for the better.
>
> Jared Spataro, CVP at Microsoft 365

Toxic culture was the #1 reason for resignations

A 2022 study found that toxic corporate culture is 10.4 times more powerful than compensation in predicting a company's attrition rate compared with its industry. Money was #16 (Sull et al., 2022).

The Covid-19 pandemic intensified and sped up the negative effects of a leadership style that focused more on the bottom line than on people. Eventually, poor mental health conditions and burnout from overwhelming responsibilities resulted in the resignation of millions of employees (Miller, 2022).

The trend went global. In Japan, Germany and Spain employees resigned or were set to resign due to mental strain or the belief that employers did not care about them (Mellor, 2022; Orvits, 2022). In addition:

- Forty-one percent of the entire global workforce reported that they were considering handing in their resignation (Microsoft work trend index, 2021)

- Similarly, in UK and Ireland 38% of employees were planning to leave their jobs in the next six months to a year (Personio & Opinium, 2021)
- Employee influence grew in Singapore: 51% set to quit jobs for better pay, career opportunities and flexibility (EY, 2022)

Among the leading elements contributing to toxic cultures are failure to promote diversity, equity and inclusion; workers feeling disrespected; and that they are the recipients of unethical behavior. The comments from four individuals below provided during personal interviews with people working to prevent Covid-19 infections provide a sense of why people resigned.

- *"I resigned because I could no longer work under my boss."*
- *"This is a very important topic – the pressures are growing and in my conversations I keep hearing that employees wish to leave and change the ways they work, but often are afraid to do so, because of the uncertainty due to Covid-19. So while in the past some would have walked away, now they keep staying and eventually burning out before removing themselves."*

The resignation statistics in education, healthcare and among women signify these groups all suffered so much that their only way out was to resign. I struggled with how to talk about the human suffering that was revealed to me in my interviews and conversations during the Covid-19 pandemic. People worried that their story would be recognized and they would suffer consequences.

The pressures at work are mounting and many employees still wish to leave and change their working lifestyle. Women, healthcare workers, teachers of all generations resigned. Some were afraid to leave because of job uncertainty. Yet others left their jobs because the work environment was too toxic for them. Of course there are stories of those who just kept going. We have not seen the end of the resignations. And, if changes are not made, I am convinced that we will be confronted with massive mental health issues exacerbated by the pandemic.

Women, teachers and healthcare workers leaving the workplace

According to the U.S. Bureau of Labor Statistics, the response to Covid-19 wasn't mentioned as frequently as other reasons for quitting. This could be because the pandemic only exacerbated the negative conditions that existed previously.

Amongst the wave of resignations, workers have an increasing desire to feel supported, seen and cared for by their managers. Attention to the wellbeing of employees demonstrates the care and compassion, many employees debate as they contemplate their desire to work:

> My perspective on jobs has definitely changed and I am no longer willing to take just anything, mental health and resources have to be part of the conversation.

Safety Advisor

Senior level women are more likely than senior level men to participate in D&I activities

Diversity & Inclusion in senior leadership	% of leaders
I listen actively to the personal stories of women of color about bias and mistreatment	**63% women** 42% men
I think carefully about my own biases about women of color	**63% women** 53% men
I publicly acknowledge or give credit to women of color for their ideas and work	**60% women** 44% men
I mentor or sponsor one or more women of color	**38% women** 23% men

Women in the workplace, Lean In; Org and McKinsey & Co., 2020

Figure 2 Senior-level women are more likely to be actively inclusive.

Women are still waiting for promotion and child care

In the United States up to 2 million women are considering leaving the workforce and businesses cannot afford it. The millions of women waiting to be promoted to manager are still waiting. Black women are dealing with long-standing issues of racial bias—and getting less support from managers and coworkers. One in three mothers have considered leaving the workforce or downshifting their careers because of Covid-19 (McKinsey Report, 2021).

The financial consequences of losing so many women could be significant. McKinsey's 2021 research shows that company profits and share performance can be close to 50% higher when women are well represented at the top. This loss in profit may be related to other findings that women are the most likely to be involved in inclusion and diversity activities. For example, the highest levels of stress and burnout during the pandemic were in the senior women executive ranks due to their effort to support employees, especially women of color.

Figure 2, Senior management level women are more likely to be actively inclusive, demonstrates that women take the most active role in creating an inclusive workplace. Having a significant number of them leave the workplace could have very negative consequences on work performance and employee wellbeing.

Healthcare workers quit in droves

About one in five healthcare workers has left their job since the pandemic started.

> Health-care workers aren't quitting because they can't handle their jobs. They're quitting because they can't handle being unable to do their jobs. Even before Covid-19, many of them struggled to bridge the gap between

the noble ideals of their profession and the realities of its business. The pandemic simply pushed them past the limits of that compromise.

(Yong, 2021)

Between 35% and 54% of American nurses and physicians felt burned out before the pandemic. During this time many have taken stock of their difficult working conditions and inadequate pay and decided that, instead of being resigned, they will simply resign (Yong, 2021).

Teacher retention is a global crisis

Teacher shortages are a global problem (Clare, 2022; Coch, 2022; Teller Report, 2022). Between recruitment difficulties and resignations, Europe lacks teachers. In England almost half plan to quit within five years because of unmanageable workloads, stress and the low levels of trust that the public and government have in teachers (The Guardian, 2022).

Teachers are the most burned out workers in America. A national survey found that 55% of teachers planned to exit earlier than anticipated. The numbers were highest among Black (62%) and Latino (59%) educators. As staff shortages deepen across the country and workload increases, more educators are feeling burned out and demoralized (Birmingham, 2022; Walker, 2022).

Teaching was a stressful occupation long before the coronavirus disease Covid-19 pandemic occurred; during the pandemic, it became even more stressful. Teachers were navigating unfamiliar technology, balancing multiple modes of teaching and concerns about returning to in-person instruction. In addition, many teachers had to care for their own children while teaching. Teachers were more likely to report experiencing frequent job-related stress and symptoms of depression than the general population.

The experiences of those likely to resign were similar to those of teachers who left the profession after the start of the pandemic. These similarities suggest that those who are undecided will quit their jobs if challenging working conditions aren't resolved to support teacher wellbeing.

Most senior leaders plan to join the great resignation

An unexpected turn of events that further supports the notion that we are in a transformational time is that according to global studies, most senior leaders plan to join the great resignation (Hatfield et al., 2022; Kelly OCG, 2022).

Many senior executives are dissatisfied in their role and lack confidence in their employer. More than half of senior leaders worldwide (58%) are unhappy in their current position, and 72% plan to leave their employer within the next two years. This loss of experienced leadership will have significant implications for companies and the global economy.

This turn of events has implications for how companies can successfully implement the change initiatives to address the present crisis. Typically every initiative begins with "senior leadership commitment." This place is a heavy load on senior executives that results in burnout. Alternatives are explored in Chapter 6, People centered change management.

Diversity and inclusion implementation and effectiveness

Inclusion is the act of making a person part of a group, where each member is afforded the same rights and opportunities. It has a direct impact on whether people feel a sense of belonging, feel heard and feel safe to express themselves authentically.

Workplace diversity is the range of human differences present within a company, including but not limited to race, ethnicity, gender identity, sexual orientation, age, physical and social class.

Many organizations responded to the Black Lives Matter movement by publishing a public statement on their position supporting equity, inclusion and diversity. Partly it was a response to political pressures from the consumer base. The other part was the recognition that a global market demanded a culturally diverse workforce. The Boston Consulting Group published a 2022 article about the benefits of inviting other nationalities into your company and executive levels. The not-so-subtle message is that this only pertains to highly skilled individual contributors.

> Reducing the obstacles to global migration, and building bridges to opportunity for talented people regardless of where they were born or what their circumstances might be, is a moral cause that also has a strong business case. The war in Ukraine, along with ongoing conflicts in Afghanistan, Syria, and elsewhere, reminds us that not all migration is voluntary—which only makes the moral cause that much more urgent.
>
> BCG (2022)

Progress is slow in the implementation of DEIB

Only one-third have implemented innovative initiatives to improve DEI, such as advocacy groups and support programs (and only 19% provide DEI training for leaders). And, studies show that many of the initiatives fail to achieve their objectives (Kelly OCG, 2022).

Progress on inclusion and diversity is slow. In 2018 a group of experts on bias, technology, discrimination and organizational design convened to focus on what is working DEIB. They pointed to two barriers. The first was that if managers are not involved in the inception planning, it did not work.

The second was the fear of retaliation, which I often hear employees talk about. They stated,

> ...approximately half of all discrimination and harassment complaints lead to some type of retaliation. And workers who complain about

harassment are more likely to end up facing career challenges or experiencing worse mental and physical health compared to similar workers who were harassed but did not complain about it.

Diversity Network (2023)

It appears that the social pressure to end discrimination and harassment is not strong enough to change this behavior. The article makes a strong case to replace legalistic mechanisms with Employee Assistance Plans (EAPs), ombuds offices and transformative dispute resolution systems. It seems that EAPs are seldom used to handle these types of situations. Yet they can be more effective because they are frequently run by vendors who are outside the system.

This makes sense because I can't think of anything more detrimental to any inclusion and belonging effort than experiencing retaliation after the promise of protection. *Psychological safety* is not the only essential element, but it is a critical one:

> Building psychological safety in an organization is only one – albeit, important – element of an effective, iterative, learning-oriented approach to change. A set of interrelated goals related to hiring, training, promoting, and learning must go hand in hand with efforts to shift the workplace climate.

Amy Edmondson (2020)

Why diversity and inclusion initiatives fall short

Diversity and inclusion are often seen as an initiative owned by a chief diversity officer or HR. We're seeing more organizations challenge this belief, and embed diversity and inclusion into the everyday work of the organization. For example, rather than running a Diversity and Inclusion Survey as a standalone initiative, companies are incorporating these concepts into engagement surveys and the action process that follows.

For various motives companies launch diversity and inclusion initiatives. Some because they believe all humans are created equal and deserve the same opportunities. Some because they understand the business value of diverse minds and experience. Others because they feel pressured by shifting societal attitudes toward integration and equity.

Nevertheless, over the past three decades in more than 800 US firms, mandatory diversity schemes made organizations less diverse. Apparently, managers had resisted hiring diversely just to affirm their autonomy (Dobbin & Kalev, 2016). And, in spite of multiple studies showing the financial benefits of a diverse management team, not much has changed in many corporations. Twenty five years later diversity has not increased at the executive level where it can make the most difference according to a study by the Boston group (2020).

Statistics show that business leadership is not growing more diverse, especially at the most senior levels; rather, the percentages of leaders from underrepresented racial and ethnic groups have hardly changed. In 2018, for example, Black managers represented only 3.3% of senior management in the US, down slightly from 3.6% in 2007 (UNC Pembroke, 2021).

The BCG study titled *The Real Reason Diversity is Lacking at the Top*, disclosed the poor corporate mentoring and executive development offerings for high potential minorities. Corporate leaders do not understand the executive development needs of minorities. They conclude that marginalized people suffer from a weak sense of belonging and have difficulty navigating professional environments. That description makes the victims sound like the problem. They can't fit in because *they* have a "weak sense of belonging?" What about, *they* won't help them fit in because they have a weak sense of how to be inclusive? (Dean, 2020)

Perhaps the executives who are comfortable in their position think the newcomers should make their own way. If they don't, then they prove that they don't have what it takes. I was in a conversation with a group of attorneys from one of the most prestigious firms in Los Angeles. One of them told me that they had hired two young black attorneys who graduated from Princeton. The two of them attended the Black Lives Matter demonstration and were arrested. So now they were in danger of losing their license to practice law. He wondered why they would risk their careers like that when they had it made.

I told them I could think of a couple of reasons. One is that they became disillusioned when they discovered that after all their hard work and making it to the "top," they were still outsiders. The other reason is that they might have wanted to demonstrate so that others like them could have full access to opportunity. I was met by silence at the table so maybe they considered what I had said.

There are arguments to invest effort and resources into building a culture that creates a sense of belonging and into helping minorities learn how to navigate the professional environment. But the reason they need help isn't because of a weak sense of belonging. They know they don't belong. For minority candidates acquiring a deeper understanding of interpersonal risk and how to navigate it is what they need.

Before we can do any work to make a community more inclusive and equitable, we need to recognize what social identities we hold and the assumptions we make about other people's identity. Understanding and respecting social identity is critical to the leader that wishes employees to be proud of where they work.

In the workplace social identities could include job roles, generation, ethnicity, race, religion, gender, sexual orientation, nationality, profession and socioeconomic status. So everyone has multiple social identities that are a part of who they are. To the extent that a person feels recognized, accepted and respected just as they are, the more likely they are to see themselves as belonging to a group or organization.

Coming to terms with our biases

We don't know what we don't know. I have a deep understanding of what it means to be blind to reality and how difficult that made it for me to excel at anything. Chains strengthened over the centuries hold back the intellectual capacity of anyone viewed as less capable whether it be because of race, gender or economic status. I could say these chains don't have to hold anyone back because they are made of thoughts. Yet, it does no good to deny their presence. It is the opposite. Denial makes them invisible and therefore stronger.

I am somewhat of an expert in recognizing bias. I lived in Mexico as a child which wasn't easy because I was born in the USA and the people around me hated the USA. Then my mom remarried and I was adopted by a racist violent white man who taught me to hate myself and all people of color. We lived in a white low-income neighborhood but the only schools I could attend were all white racist upper-class schools.

I attended an all upper middle class white high school from 1965 to 1968 where there was no mention of racism or inequality for women. We learned about women gaining the right to vote, but it never occurred to me to question why we didn't have it in the first place. Instead I felt it was natural to have to fight for these rights, and luckily we lived in a democracy that allowed us to do it. Unfortunately, I did not recognize the pattern in the civil rights movement that was in full swing. We never discussed it in our classes and I did not identify with the protesters in spite of the fact that some of the students called me a nigger behind my back.

I am not sure if surviving all of that makes me a remarkable individual or a crazy one. Suffice it to say that it is the foundation for all my work. As a teacher and later as an organizational development consultant I saw myself as providing the strategies, knowledge and skills to accomplish goals. But beyond that I helped people work past their self-imposed limitations based on what other people thought of them. I found this to be true even amongst the highest levels of the organization, but particularly with minority women, managers and executives.

As a university student I decided to do a special project on the removal of the Cherokee Nation from their native lands to Oklahoma. It was my first exposure to the horrific cruelty of the US government. Thousands of Native Americans died on the trek. I was so stunned that I could not digest the implications of my research. Or that Americans could be capable of such cruelty. In Mexico I had learned about the Spanish greed and inhumaneness when they colonized the Americas. In the States I was taught that Americans were different, just and generous. The professor gave me a B+ because my research was original, but he said I had failed to offer an analysis of the historical meaning of that event. I had no idea what he meant. I was terrified to see myself reflected in those events either as a perpetrator or victim.

I share this story to reveal my own shortcomings. Our education plays a large role in concealing our biases from us. Implicit biases are habitual responses that stem from cultural learnings. They are a byproduct of our socialization and not east moral failing. When we are not aware of them, our habits are activated producing and undesired results. Unfortunately we may not even connect our actions with those results.

Opportunities for change

The resignations left a different kind of pandemic in their wake. Oppressive workloads and burnout could trigger new disasters because exhausted teams would not have the capacity to prevent them. An essential employee reported the difficulties of home service calls:

> There was high stress going into people's houses during a pandemic- no additional pay- during the beginning of the pandemic, we were on essential service only – But during the height of Covid-19 deaths we switched back to standard full service- Added responsibility was never compensated. The shortage of staff company-wide should show that the work is too taxing and the compensation is negligible. Taking care of customers is solely supported by the dedication and vigilance of honorable workers. The safety of our community, customers, employees, and the company relies on overworked under compensated fatigued skeleton crews.

Employees have experienced a great deal of turmoil in the last couple of decades. As the cost of living has increased significantly, their salaries have not. Couple that with rising demands. Teachers face a wider range of cultures with fewer resources. Women face rising childcare costs that they cannot pay based on current wages. Nearly one in four teachers said that they were likely to leave their jobs by the end of the 2020–2021 school year. Black or African American teachers were particularly likely to plan to leave.

Is servant leadership a way to stem the resignations?

One study of 1,120 teachers within a kindergarten to 12th-grade public school explored the relationship between school principals with servant leader behaviors and the impact on teacher retention, teacher job satisfaction and principal efficacy. It was found that servant leadership has a statistically significant positive effect on teacher retention. Empowerment is the most effective behavior to retain teachers. Other findings included specific professional development opportunities.

The results of this study resemble the psychological safety Edmondson studies. Autonomy and professional development opportunities are two salient aspects of high-performance teams.

Other research shows that school leaders who protect teachers' time, invite their input and support their mental health and wellbeing through comprehensive programs see higher levels of satisfaction. Unions continue to push districts to address shortages, reduce the extreme demand on educators and hire more health and wellness coordinators (Walker, 2021).

These are opportunities for leaders to look at what they are asking people to do. Let's eliminate the parts of the job that are not as important. Give people choices in the kinds of work they do. There is incredible power in giving people work that they find meaningful and important. Give managers and supervisors the learning opportunities to develop the skills to support employees effectively. But most importantly, leaders will have to provide far better mental health support than they have in the past.

It will take strategic approaches from multiple disciplines to recover from this crisis. All entail alignment with the human side of organization to be successful. Developing trust and open communication in an organization involves psycho-emotional involvement from leaders it will also take emphasizing psychological safety and the mitigation of psychosocial hazards.

Detecting and releasing bias

I believe that the biases I internalized during my childhood conflicted with my ability to process the new information I was learning. Implicit biases are essentially bad habits that stem from cultural learnings—they are a byproduct of our socialization and not a moral failing. If we are not aware of our biases, those habits can become activated and applied by default even when they may be undesirable and counteract our intentions. Recognizing them and letting them go it's not a one-time exercise.

Bibliography

Anjum, Z. (2021). Hybrid work is the next big disruption. Accessed July 14, 2022. https://www.linkedin.com/pulse/hybrid-work-next-big-disruption-zubair-anjum/

Birmingham, K. (2022). K-12 workers are the most burned out employees in America, and it's a sign the teacher shortage will intensify. *Fortune*. https://fortune.com/2022/06/15/teachers-burnout-workers-quitting-great-resignation/

Catalyst. (2021). *The great work life divide*. Accessed August 12, 2022. https://www.catalyst.org/research/flexibility-demand-future-of-work/

Clare, J. (2022). Teacher workforce shortages issues paper. https://ministers.education.gov.au/clare/teacher-workforce-shortages-issues-paper

Coch, L. (2022). Teacher shortages are a global problem. https://theconversation.com/teacher-shortages-are-a-global-problem-prioritising-australian-visas-wont-solve-ours-189468

Dean, J. (2020). The real reason diversity is lacking at the top. *BCG*. https://www.bcg.com/publications/2020/why-is-diversity-lacking-at-top-of-corporations?utm_medium=Email&utm_source=esp&utm_campaign=none&utm_description=ealert&utm_topic=none&utm_geo=global&utm_content=202012&utm_usertoken=2b0726e1a3875436b177b482209d071a74a19c4e

Dean, J., Rice, J., Williams, W., Pineros, B., Acosta, D., Pancham, I., & Snelgrove, M. (2020). The real reason diversity is lacking at the top. Accessed May 26, 2022. https://www.bcg.com/publications/2020/why-is-diversity-lacking-at-top-of-corporations

Diversity Network (2023). 5 recommendations for improving your D&I efforts. https://diversity-network.com/5-recommendations-for-improving-your-di-efforts/

Dobbin, F., & Kalev, A. (2016). Why diversity programs fail. *Harvard Business Review*. Accessed July 15, 2022. https://hbr.org/2016/07/why-diversity-programs-fail

Edmondson, A. (2020). The role of psychological safety in diversity and inclusion: Without it, true DIB is even more of a challenge. *Psychology Today*. Accessed May 1, 2022. https://www.psychologytoday.com/us/blog/the-fearless-organization/202006/the-role-psychological-safety-in-diversity-and-inclusion#:~:text=I%20am%20not%20arguing%20that,learning%2Doriented%20approach%20to%20change

EY. (2022). Accessed August 12, 2022. https://www.ey.com/en_sg/news/2022/07/employee-influence-in-singapore-grows-51-percentage-set-to-quit-jobs-for-better-pay-career-opportunities-and-flexibility

Guardian. (2022). Unmanageable' workloads, stress and levels of trust in teachers from public and government key factors. https://www.theguardian.com/education/2022/apr/11/teachers-england-plan-to-quit-workloads-stress-trust

Harnoss, J. D., Schwarz, A., Candelon, F., Reeves, M., Grice A., Kimura, R., & Lang, N. (2022). When innovation has no borders culture is key. Accessed July 12, 2022. https://www.bcg.com/publications/2022/innovation-without-borders?utm_medium=Email&utm_source=esp&utm_campaign=none&utm_description=ealert&utm_topic=none&utm_geo=Global&utm_content=202207&utm_usertoken=2b0726e1a3875436b177b482209d071a74a19c4e

Hatfield, S., Fisher, J., & Silvergate, P. G. (2022). C-Suite's role in wellbeing. *Deloitte*. Accessed July 1, 2022. https://www2.deloitte.com/us/en/insights/topics/leadership/employee-wellness-in-the-corporate-workplace.html?id=us:2sm:3li:4diUS175466:5awa::MMDDYY::author&pkid=1008950

Kelly OCG. (2022). The looming threat of boss loss: Most senior leaders plan to join the great resignation. *Global Survey Finds*. https://www.kellyservices.com/global/about-us/news-center/news-releases/ocg/2022/the-looming-threat-of-boss-loss-most-senior-leaders-plan-to-join-the-great-resignation-global-survey-finds/

Lavaza, A., & Garasic, M. D. (2022). What is some patients are more important than others? *BMC Medical Ethics*. Accessed August 13, 2022. https://bmcmedethics.biomedcentral.com/articles/10.1186/s12910-022-00763-2

McKensie & Co. (2021). Women in the workplace. https://www.mckinsey.com/featured-insights/diversity-and-inclusion/women-in-the-workplace

McKinsey Report. (2021). Diversity wins. https://www.mckinsey.com/featured-insights/diversity-and-inclusion/diversity-wins-how-inclusion-matters

Mellor, S. (2022). Pandemic driven depression is driving labor shortages. *Fortune Magazine*. Accessed May 14, 2022. https://fortune.com/2022/01/21/Covid-19-pandemic-driven-depression-world-labor-shortage/

Microsoft work trend index. (2021). Accessed July 14, 2022. https://www.microsoft.com/en-us/worklab/work-trend-index/hybrid-work

Miller, A. (2022). The A&M professor that predicted the great resignation explains potential factors of why that theory came true. *The Eagle*. Accessed August 12, 2022. https://theeagle.com/news/a_m/a-m-professor-who-predicted-great-resignation-explains-potential-factors-of-why-theory-came-true/article_e99bb37c-6f29-11ec-9a2e-030d1c45b621.html

National Academies of Sciences, Engineering, and Medicine. (2019). *Taking action against clinician burnout: A systems approach to professional wellbeing.* The National Academies Press: Washington, DC.

Orvits, K. (2022). Worker retention starts with easing employee stress and strain. Accessed March 1, 2022. https://ohsonline.com/articles/2022/02/01/worker-retention-starts-with-easing-employee-stress-and-strain.aspx

Pedulla, D. (2020). Diversity and inclusion efforts that really work. *Harvard Business Review.* Accessed August 29, 2022. https://hbr.org/2020/05/diversity-and-inclusion-efforts-that-really-work

Personio & Opinium. (2021). Counting the cost: How businesses risk a post pandemic talent drain. https://hr.personio.de/hubfs/EN_Downloads/202104_HRStudy_UKI.pdf

Sull, D., Sull, C., & Zweig, B. (2022). Toxic culture is driving the great resignation. Accessed May 16, 2022. https://sloanreview.mit.edu/article/toxic-culture-is-driving-the-great-resignation/

Teller Report. (2022). Between recruitment difficulties and resignations. *Europe Flex Teachers.* https://www.tellerreport.com/news/2022-08-26-between-recruitment-difficulties-and-resignations--europe-lacks-teachers.BJbM-3VIyo.html

UNC Pembroke. (2021). Why diversity and inclusion are good for business. https://online.uncp.edu/articles/mba/diversity-and-inclusion-good-for-business.aspx

Walker, T. (2021). Getting serious about teacher burnout. Accessed August 8, 2022. https://www.nea.org/advocating-for-change/new-from-nea/getting-serious-about-teacher-burnout

Walker, T. (2022). An alarming number of educators may soon leave the profession. Accessed August 8, 2022. https://www.nea.org/advocating-for-change/new-from-nea/survey-alarming-number-educators-may-soon-leave-profession

Weisenthal, J., & Alloway, T. (2021). How the black death pandemic reshaped Europe's feudal economy. *Bloomberg.* Accessed July 14, 2022. https://www.bloomberg.com/news/articles/2021-01-09/how-the-black-death-pandemic-reshaped-europe-s-feudal-economy

Wiles, J. (2022). Employees seek personal value and purpose at work. Be prepared to deliver it. Accessed March 1, 2022. https://www.gartner.com/en/articles/employees-seek-personal-value-and-purpose-at-work-be-prepared-to-deliver-1?source=BLD-200123&utm_medium=social&utm_source=bambu&utm_campaign=SM_GB_YOY_GTR_SOC_BU1_SM-BA-SWG

Yong, E. (2021). Why health-care workers are quitting in droves. Accessed April 6, 2022. https://www.theatlantic.com/health/archive/2021/11/the-mass-exodus-of-americas-health-carworkers/620713/

4 Psychosocial risk and mental health

- The mental health crisis is growing
- Recognizing and addressing psychological injuries in the workplace
- Discrimination and classism as a psychosocial hazards
- The risks of a Hybrid workplace

The International Organization for Standardization (ISO) has put psycho-social hazards (PSHs) on the dashboard as a workplace safety management responsibility. ISO 45003:2021[1]: opens the way for feelings and emotions to be taken seriously in the workplace. And, yes, that includes inclusion and belonging.

PSHs are factors in the design or management of work that increase the risk of work-related stress and can lead to psychological or physical harm. Examples of work-related PSHs might include poor supervisor support or high job demands. They also include unsupportive peer-to-peer behaviors and attitudes. PSHs carry both physical and emotional risks for the workplace as a whole. The PSHs people experienced during the pandemic led to a mental health crisis (WorkSafe Australia, 2022).

Other hazards include discrimination, gender bias, and classism.

Just as a lack of focus on mitigating physical, chemical, biological, ergonomic, or safety hazards can lead to bodily injury or death. Similarly, a lack of focus on PSH's can cause emotional wounds, cripple performance, limit potential, and severely damage not only the team but the individuals on a team (Clark, 2020).

Some safety professionals ask, "Why concentrate on psychological aspects of the workplace when people are still sticking their hands into machinery?" While I empathize with the frustration, this reaction shows a lack of understanding regarding social and human factors. It also points out the long road ahead if we expect not only safety advisors but supervisors to adopt the concepts of psychological safety and psychosocial injuries.

Worldwide 750,000 deaths linked to long hours each year

Nearly half of the entire workforce, 44% of workers are feeling burnout on the job. This is up from just 34% in 2020. Over half of all employers, 52%

DOI: 10.4324/9781003368724-4

are expecting workplace disruptions due to drug and alcohol-related issues in the coming year. Nearly 1/3 of all employers are experiencing financial impacts, in some cases severe financial impacts, due to mental health related issues (Pandley, 2021).

The WHO and ILO (2021) reported that 2 million people died in work-related causes each year. The study considered 19 occupational risk factors and found that the key risk was exposure to long hours, which is a PSH. About 750,000 deaths were linked to long hours. They also reported that the prevalence of global mental health problems increased in 2021 and the services available to help do not meet existing levels of demand.

Our society has made significant progress in the areas of employee safety, health and fairness in the workplace. The conversation taking place around improving inclusion, belonging and diversity in many countries is a recognition that the way people feel at work affects their quality of life, mental and physical health.

That said when it comes to safety and health, companies lack robust mental health support and primarily focus on physical hazards. This is despite data that psychological injuries are on the rise (Canadian Occupational Safety, 2021). Experts are growing ever more concerned as the numbers associated with mental health issues continue to rise.

Work-related PSH and risk examples

Individuals under stress at work may end up developing health problems. These negative effects have consequences on the whole organization and in society. They can lead to irritability and violence in the workplace. They can lower performance and increase accidents. Psychosocial risks can generate anxiety, depression, apathy, which can restrict the ability to concentrate or to make decisions. At the societal level we see rising health costs and decreased financial stability that leads to increased crime and homelessness.

PSHs can be present in all organizations regardless of the nature of the work. These hazards fall into the themes as shown in Table 1, PSHs in the workplace. As the risk column indicates these hazards can have both personal and business negative consequences.

Other psychosocial stressors can include divorce, the death of a child, prolonged illness, unwanted change of residence, a natural catastrophe, or a highly competitive work situation.

The relationship between management and employees as a PSH

In *Managing the Unexpected*, Karl Weick and Sutcliffe (2009) examines the 1984 Bhopal disaster from a psychosocial perspective. While the incident was the result of physical failures, Weick suggests that the neglect of the physical facilities began with the mentality engendered by senior leadership.

Table 1 Psychosocial hazards (PSHs) in the workplace

Workplace PSHs	Psychosocial emotional hazards	Psychosocial risks	Preventative actions
Voicing disagreement, concerns or new ideas	Stress	Exclusion	Insist on disagreement and listen
Job demands	Difficulties when combining labor and personal responsibilities	Poor family/life balance	Ask direct reports (DRs) about their health and offer flex schedules
Workload and work pace	Discrimination	Poor mental health	Inquire about stress levels and even out workload
Poor management of changes	Job or financial insecurity	Stress of uncertainty	Provide timely and correct information
Lack of job control or autonomy	Lack of career development	Talent resignation	Explain the why for changes; increase autonomy.
Unclear priorities and expectations	Disagreement in interpersonal relations	Mistakes and business failure	Always clarify priorities; agree on expectations and timelines.
Lack of support by the supervisor or co-worker	Lack of recognition, respect and appreciation	Decrease of employee engagement	Make personal development a priority and listening
Aspects of the work environment such as equipment and hazardous tasks	Harassment, aggression and violence	Physical or psychological injury	Ask frequently, "how can I help?" Show that both psychological and physical injuries are important.

A former project engineer said, "The plant was losing money, and top management decided that saving money was more important than safety (Weick: 232)." An assumption that took over site management was that the plant was unimportant. The Bhopal employees knew how unimportant they were to management as they watched the plant go into disrepair.

Those with less power felt the disregard for their lives and consequences most acutely. Not only was maintenance poor, but employees also felt that their unit didn't matter. This resulted in indifference, increased turnover and "work to rule," which led to constructing a reality of disheartened workers with a loss of control over the technology that made it harder for errors to be contained.

Top management's perceptions of Bhopal set into motion enactments that confirmed their perceptions. It became a self-fulfilling prophecy that resulted in over 500,000 people being exposed to a highly toxic gas, 3,787 deaths and 574,366 injured (Mandavilli, 2018).

So psychosocial injuries can trigger behaviors that lead to disasters. They can also trigger personal injuries by lowering situational awareness. According to Dr. I. David Daniels (2021) Black workers experience higher physical injury rates as well as higher exposure to discrimination. Since there is a direct correlation between psychosocial and physical injury as well as rehabilitation time after an injury. "… it is logical to conclude that a higher incidence of physical injuries is likely masking exposure to a significant number of PSHs" (Daniels, 2021: 10–11).

Racial, gender and social class discrimination as PSHs

Ethnic minority groups across the world face a complex set of adverse social and psychological challenges, often involving racial discrimination. It is an important contributing factor to health disparities among non–dominant ethnic minorities (Fani et al., 2021). These are health issues that show substantial similarities to chronic social stress. The same outcomes apply to many groups such as Asian Americans, Indigenous Australians and ethnic minority groups in the UK.

Discrimination is usually accompanied by exclusion. When people feel excluded or disrespected in the workplace wellbeing goes down as well as engagement and productivity. This is by no means a problem that only affects people of color. It does affect them more frequently as the data will show but almost everyone has felt excluded.

The feeling of exclusion is so normal that psychologists have difficulty in defining how much is abnormal. The problem of exclusion is not qualitative it's quantitative. We may all experience exclusion the same, but how often determines the overall effect on our wellbeing and opportunities for advancement.

There is no difference between social pain and physical pain. Exclusion results in a psychosocial injury that can manifest as depression, anxiety or a physical ailment. Most of the experimental studies investigating the neural pathways of social exclusion used a ball tossing game (cyberball). Participants played a video game in which they played with two computer-controlled players who they believed were other human participants (Eisenberger et al., 2003). During the course of the game the participant is then either included by the computer players or excluded from the game by not receiving any ball contacts. Self-reported distress due to exclusion showed up in the same part of the brain that signals physical pain. When everyone was included there was no activity in brain regions linked to distress and social pain (Masten et al., 2013). Those who suffered exclusion during the experiment were given Tylenol and reported relief from their social pain.

People who report feeling "unseen or unheard" use a great deal of energy to survive psychically and physically. The Covid-19 stories in this book speak to the fact that this marginalization extends to professions as well as ethnicity or gender. Safety professionals, nurses, teachers and essential workers felt the brunt of the pandemic and continue to feel it. Not only does this cause a lot of suffering, it also robs society of so much creativity and contribution.

Latinx and Black American workers experience discrimination equally

The extent of the problem is serious. An 8,000 person study by the Gallup Center on Black Voices found 24% of both Black and Latinx respondents reported experiencing workplace discrimination, far higher than the portion of white respondents (15%). Age appeared to be a notable factor as well: 31% of workers in both groups younger than 40 said they'd experienced discrimination in the last year, nearly twice the percentage of those over the age of 40 (17%). It is possible that the younger workers were experiencing ageism as well as racial discrimination.

Black and Latinx workers suffer discrimination and lack of respect equally (Lloyd 2021). This is an important factor to consider when providing services because often Latinx workers are quiet and can be overlooked. Compared to the research on Black Americans in the USA, there is very little on the Latinx workforce experience concerning psychosocial injury. This is of concern because Latinx worker numbers are growing and their fatal and non-fatal occupational injuries are higher than any other ethnic group. A 2009 study also found that Latinx work-related illness, injury or assault were associated with experiences of racial harassment or discrimination (Shannon et al., 2009).

Gender discrimination

Gender discrimination is referred to as sexism, and "occurs when employers make decisions such as selection, evaluation, promotion, or reward allocation on the basis of an individual's gender" (Lloyd-Jones et al., 2018). However in my experience, most of the bias is unconscious.

Gender issues are more prominent as more women enter the workforce. It is bigger than race or any other differences addressed by initiatives seeking to recognize and embrace diversity under the auspices of globalization and the need for marketplace innovation. One of the areas that comes up frequently in safety and health is the hazard mitigation for pregnant women. In one focus group a woman who works in a lab was concerned about how the chemical agents she was working with would affect her pregnancy. She did not get a response from the H&S manager for eight months.

There is another important form of gender discrimination. Often excluded from workplace diversity discussions are issues involving lesbian, gay, bisexual, transgender, queer, and other non-heterosexual (LGBTQ+) individuals. This is a complex issue in which I have no expertise. I believe it is best to refer the reader to Chaney and Hawley's excellent article, *Developing Human Resource Development Competencies to Manage Sexual Orientation and Transgender* (Chaney & Hawley, 2018).

Classism as a PSH

Having conducted hundreds of organizational assessments during my 30-year career, I have noticed a disturbing commonality. Individual contributors/managers consistently show that they experience a much higher quality of work life than hourly employees. An example would be the percent of agreement on statements such as, "I have been thanked for my work at least once in the last three months." Given what we know about the human need for recognition, a 70% agreement from the individual contributors versus a 40% agreement from hourly would indicate these groups were having very different experiences at work.

Another example of this gap was in a 2021 Global study (Figure 3) where 61% of leaders describe themselves as "thriving." Yet, those without decision-making authority were 23% points lower Gen Z, frontline workers, newer employees and single people struggled the most (Work Trend Index, 2021).

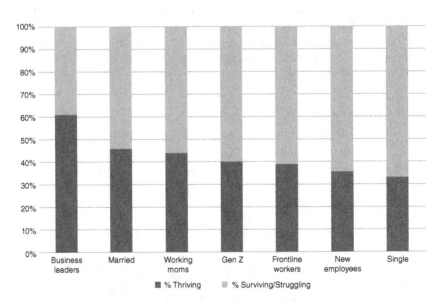

Figure 3 The Work Trend Index survey (Microsoft Worklab, 2021), was conducted by an independent research firm, Edelman Data Intelligence, of 31,092 full-time employed or self-employed workers across 31 markets—between January 12, 2021 and January 25, 2021.

What is classism?

Classism refers to the differential treatment based on social class or perceived social class. Social class in the working environment is not necessarily based on economics. For example, sometimes operators in nuclear and utilities industry can make more money than managers. The larger salary, however does not qualify them for inclusion in the higher power class at work.

There is a largely unconscious bias around class that operates in the workplace, how it manifests and the self-perception of social class status. Status is typically determined by role, how much money a person makes and the years of education completed. Based on those factors, job roles could be assigned social status. This enabled the analysis of safety culture surveys taken over the past 30 years for insight into employee perceptions based on social class.

The social class terminology serves as an analogy to describe classism in the workplace. The upper and upper middle classes represent varying degrees of power. These are generally the executives, managers and valued individual contributors. The middle and working classes experience less inequality than the lower classes. To assign work roles to categories I used a study that utilized salary ranges and asked employees to self-describe their social class.

The middle class are composed of supervisors and skilled employees. But, being in the same class does not mean that supervisors and mechanics would see themselves as part of the same social field. The working classes are made up of hourly, contractors and temporary workers. Lower classes would be migrant or seasonal labor. In my experience permanent employees do not see themselves as being treated as well as supervisors, but they feel they have a higher status than contractors.

Power does play a role in how satisfied people are with the status quo. The next section looks at the consequences of classism and how it shows up in the workplace as lack of caring and respect.

Classism and respect in the workplace

Classism leads to treating people with more or less respect based on their class status and value. While people accept differentials in power, they still need to be respected as human beings and for their contributions. When they are not there is little motivation to perform at their best. Worse, there is a loss of trust between levels of the organization and individuals. So lack of respect in the workplace constitutes a PSH. The risks are higher accident rates, higher absenteeism and lower employee engagement.

Managers may not realize that there exists a tacit lack of respect in the way they treat people who work in the field or the manufacturing floor versus individual contributors. For example, in one survey 56% of employees thought their company's executives cared about their wellbeing, while 91% of the C-suite thought their employees believed they care about it. That is a 35% gap, which is significant. It indicates that management is not getting as much information as they need to keep employees engaged.

Table 2 Respect perception differences between individual contributors, managers and hourly

---

"How does your company reinforce the idea that employees are viewed as the most valuable asset of the organization?"

Individual contributors/management	Hourly
Yes, I am very respected by my manager. (HR manager)	Managers can cuss employees out and threaten their jobs and the manager gets promoted!
Yes, he respects me majorly. He asks me to help solve problems and gives me challenging assignments. (Engineer)	One of the Lean instructors told us, "You people are dumb. We will ship this plant so far South your heads will spin."
I am respected all the time. It's one of the things I like about working here. (Office staff)	No, they are only interested in production.
Yes. I'm viewed as an expert in my area and they listen to me. (Engineer)	We've done this job for years and no one listens to us.
I am respected on a constant basis—I like it when my opinion is asked. (Engineer)	No, it would be nice if my boss said "Good morning."

These types of disconnects are common. Over the years safety culture assessments show hourly worker scores lower than engineering and management scores in facilities with low trust levels. The comments in Table 2 are from interviews at one manufacturing site with low engagement scores during the Covid-19 experience. They illustrate that hourly employees experience much less respect from management than knowledge workers.

Lack of respect and threats contribute to conflicts, misunderstandings and decreased performance. Uncomfortable as it may be, leaders need to recognize that these perception gaps on surveys don't just tell us how each group feels. They tell us about tangible and intangible privileges like recognition and respect that are less accessible to those of lower status.

One plant manager decided to ask what activities workers felt were a sign of respect. The number one issue was the lack of timely response to concerns and requests. "They always say, 'I will get back to you,' but they never do." Consequently management launched an "I will get back to you campaign" and focused on doing that for a year. When the survey results came back, the score on addressing concerns in a timely manner was in the positive range.

When seen in that light, new opportunities open up to close that gap. No longer are solutions restricted to improving procedures, processes and equipment. Much of what has to be done lies in the arena of improving relationships and meeting the social needs of all employees as exemplified by this hourly employee comment about their boss.

My boss is more concerned about our safety than meeting production goals. That means a lot. He is a very caring individual. As soon as we say that needs to be replaced, he does it. My team is one of the happiest groups even though (company) doesn't pay that well.

The Covid-19 pandemic was more than a physical health concern. It had deep social and psychological repercussions that have affected many organizational groups as shown in the resignation statistics. "Essential workers" bore risks during the pandemic that extended beyond the non-trivial risks of infection, psychological and physical stress to the physical, social and economic costs experienced by exposed workers.

Some workers received extra pay and lots of recognition as "heroes" during the height of the pandemic. Recent safety surveys indicate that is no longer happening. Those who have stopped the practice show a lack of knowledge about human systems. During the pandemic people enjoyed the appreciation and thank you. The height of the crisis appears to have passed, but they still feel they are fulfilling a vital function. The need for recognition and belonging does not turn on and off with an event or crisis. The following comment from hourly worker should make that point.

> ...look at the past year and a half, you (management) stayed home because of concern for yourselves! but we are your heroes, We would rather you say you don't give a crap about us than lie about it every day.

It is the same dedicated workers doing the same essential work. Let's not lose sight of the reality awakened by the pandemic. We would all suffer without their contributions. So why not always thank and recognize them?

Mitigating the psychosocial risk of discrimination

Mitigation also called coping describes the emotions, the ability to interpret and behaviors that an individual has at their disposal to ameliorate or overcome stress. Some coping skills may be perceived as negative such as raising one's voice or positive such as making self-deprecating jokes. It is a set of skills learned over a lifetime of responding to PSH exposure. I am not sure that I agree with the view that coping is a negative response while resilience is a positive response to adversity. I have observed an excess of either one can lead to burnout.

There are actions that both businesses and individuals use to mitigate discrimination. Daniels (2021) asked, "How do Black workers mitigate their exposure to recognizable PSHs?" 60% of the responses showed that the respondents felt good about the way they coped with discrimination. This suggests that individuals who recognize (PSHs) and take steps to mitigate them have a positive attitude and self-image. However, the frequency of exposure to discrimination impacts their ability to respond in this way.

> Lower-level workers are also more likely to be subjected to direct individual forms of racist and discriminatory behavior, including stereotypical slurs, direct work interference, or sabotage, as well as direct threats. Those at higher levels in the organization are likely to observe and experience more organizational discrimination than individual discrimination. These generally come in more nuanced actions or the cumulative

effect of microaggressions. (Microaggressions are subtle but offensive behaviors directed at members of marginalized groups).

(Daniels, 2021: 41)

Daniels (2021) continues that 40% of the participants assumed or accepted a sense of responsibility for their circumstances "including accepting exposure as an inevitable part of their work-life or taking action to reduce the hazard." This sense of responsibility and consequently having to take action to mitigate or avoid experiencing exclusion is exhausting and leads to burnout. Accepting responsibility is both a coping and resilience strategy.

I was in my early 30s when I decided to take responsibility in the face of conflict or discrimination by saying it was my choice to leave, try and change things or accept things as they were. Having a choice gave me a sense of control. It seemed natural to assume the responsibility for both understanding and being understood. It is one of the reasons I ended up in organizational development. I was an avid student of conflict resolution and dialog. But life kept bringing people into my experience that did not respond to the techniques I'd learned.

There is an argument over whether it takes 3 or 30 seconds for people to form an opinion of your status when you first meet. There was a lot of pain and struggle involved in trying to change people's opinions of me—to see me as a high potential. It took me a long time to come to terms with the fact that some people don't want to go past their first impressions of someone they meet. They don't want to upset the status quo, which might happen if suddenly someone you excluded turned out to be a valuable employee.

These days I am having a different experience with most people I meet. It is probably due to the increasing acceptance of differences in our society. I am certain however, that the biggest reason I am experiencing much more inclusion is that I have learned to accept myself, even like myself. I will go into more detail over my a-ha moment, but I believe that because emotions are contagious what do you think of yourself affects others around you. That does not excuse racial biases. It is merely another tool in the toolbox of those who are open to the idea.

Mitigation isn't about being able to completely protect people from discrimination. The encounters will happen as long as our society maintains hierarchies of gender, color, profession or wealth. I think we are trying to raise our awareness of how our actions, words and thoughts impact others. We are also helping people to question their assumptions and biases that lead them to treating some people differently than they treat others. This is something that should be funded at the corporate level.

The psychosocial risks of the hybrid work environment

Leaders are struggling to make hybrid work a success. Two in ten firms believe that hybrid work has a positive impact on organizational culture.

Another 66% say they are redefining their systems to include hybrid workers, only a third provide avenues to provide input (Kelly, 2022).

Ever since I interviewed essential workers during Covid-19 I have known that there were complaints about the "privileges" of the people working from home.

> I sense a growing resentment on the part of essential workers (hourly and salary) towards those who have been allowed to work remotely. As someone who has had to come to the plant every day since the start of the lockdown I feel it as well. Is there any plan to recognize or reward those of us who have been here every day, wearing masks all day long, taking time to drive in, buying gas, etc.?
>
> Hourly worker in manufacturing

At first it was assumed that when everyone returned to the office the tension would be over, but there was another drama taking place.

Remote employees preferred to work from home (Saad & Wigert, 2021). The experts say that demanding that they return to the office could cost companies their best talent. So negotiations are taking place. There will be some combination of home and office schedules.

The typical employee-executive disconnect is alive and well. A global survey of 10,000 knowledge workers revealed that executives are three times more likely to want to return to the office. The desire for flexible work policies is strongest with employees of color and with women, especially working parents. The survey also showed that 57% of the knowledge workers were open to looking for a new job (Slack, 2021).

The importance of fairness in return-to-office plans

Yale professor, Dr. Heidi Brooks, emphasizes the importance of fairness in return-to-office plans and says executives must consider the pandemic's "differential impacts," particularly around race and gender. For example, women with young children have to figure out childcare to go into work. I would add that the fairness must include the hourly employees in the warehouse or manufacturing floor. These were the "essential workers" during the pandemic, but no one is talking about them now. It would be a serious mistake not to have conversations on the floor with them to find out more about their needs and how the company may compensate them.

Interestingly, a 2021 Slack survey 21 found that 97% of Black knowledge workers in the U.S. currently working remotely want a full-time hybrid or remote option. Whereas only 33% of all men would rather not return to the workplace (The Conference Board, 2021). This makes sense to me because many minority employees may feel a greater sense of PS working from home. There they don't have to adapt their behavior or appearance, nor do they have to risk potential exclusion or discrimination.

Indeed (2021) research found that the other group that prefers working remotely is women. 74% of full-time working women (mothers or primary caregivers) say remote work helps them perform their jobs better. The Indeed article proposes that companies need to prioritize inclusion and belonging for women and any marginalized social group. Based on that data, what changes should be made to account for the diversity imbalances in the physical world place?

Psychosocial risk of isolation in remote work

Neuroscience research has found that only in-person interactions trigger the full suite of physiological responses and neural synchronization required for optimal human communication and trust-building, and that digital channels such as videoconferencing disrupt our processing of communicative information. These issues lead to the possibility that large-scale practice of remote work could result in loss of social connection, poor communication skills, fewer meaningful relationships and loss of trust (Parker et al., 2020; Yang et al., 2022).

In contrast, when employees are in the same physical space, they bump into one another in the hallway, stop by one another's desks for impromptu meetings, go out for a chat over coffee, or socialize after work. All of these interactions support the development of trust and open communication.

The biggest challenge will be keeping people engaged and connected. They require explicit leadership effort to develop virtual meeting practices that help participants feel that they are an integral part of the group, that their ideas matter, and that their perspectives are welcomed to create a sense of belonging.

The mental health during Covid-19 and after

A mental health pandemic seems to be following the Covid-19 (The Guardian, 2022). Globally, 92% of people consider mental health as important or more important than physical health for overall wellbeing (Welcome Trust. org., 2022). The pandemic had people scrambling for mental health services. Therapists reported a surge in demand for treatment of anxiety and depression, as well as trauma and stress-related disorders. Meanwhile, those seeking help were forced to wait for weeks (American psychological assoc., 2021). Millions of patients in England face dangerously long waits for mental healthcare as well. Leaders there have dubbed this the second pandemic. As bad as the situations are, they are nothing in comparison to Third World countries such as Lebanon.

The Lebanese pound has lost 81% value since 2019 while coping with a pandemic, recovering from the Beirut Port explosion, and experiencing social unrest. In some hospitals, healthcare workers were provided with defective gloves, and masks not designed for medical use. If that weren't enough, healthcare workers faced verbal abuse and attacks from patients and their families when they could not help them.

So we are in a global mental health crisis and employees expect support from employers to protect their mental health. But there seems to be more emphasis on teaching employees to be resilient than looking at how employers can be more supportive. The good news is we don't need to invent a whole new system. Per mental health expert, Georgia Bryce Hutchingson (2022):

> Worker wellbeing has always been important. It took Covid-19 to upend some things and to precipitate in the well needed conversation.
>
> Employees are not complaining about anything new. Their concerns have always been there. Perhaps organizational leaders are increasingly paying attention because the pandemic helped to put some things in perspective. Maybe leaders themselves have been affected by current happenings as their employees (a leveling of the field of some sort).
>
> 'Finding the best approach requires a thoughtful analysis of what your workers need to achieve a holistic state of wellbeing...' Workers know what they need. We simply need to listen and be more responsive. I believe the 'Great Resignation' is helping to facilitate better alignment in this regard.
>
> The mental health (MH) discourse need not involve creation or invention of a whole new experience or dogma. When workers feel respected, valued, cared for, and viewed holistically, rather than as 'cogs in a system', the natural outflow will be MH – 'state of someone functioning at a satisfactory level of cognitive. emotional, and behavioral adjustment.'
>
> Georgia Bryce Hutchingson

Burnout data during Covid-19

Several psychosocial risk factors have a significant effect on employee mental health, overall organizational health, and the financial bottom line. Table 3, Comparison of burnout rates in the workplace, displays data from a McKinsey & LeanIn.org study (2020) on women in the workplace during Covid-19 showed that some social groups experienced more psychosocial injuries than others in the world can you do that in the form of burnout. It is in sync with the resignations we are seeing in the workplace. The most serious indicator is the number of women leaving the workplace and the burnout at the senior executive level.

Many companies have not adjusted the workplace expectations that are responsible for employee stress and burnout. Less than a third of companies have modified their performance review criteria to account for challenges created by the pandemic such as child care and home schooling. That means many employees—especially parents and caregivers—are facing the choice between falling short of pre-pandemic expectations that may now be unrealistic, or pushing themselves to keep up an unsustainable pace.

As Table 3 demonstrates, that women in general had the highest stress levels. Senior leaders felt the highest level of exhaustion. Data indicates that senior

Table 3 Comparison of burnout rates in the workplace

% response	Fathers	Mothers	Sr. men leaders	Sr. women leaders	Black men	Black women
60				♣		
50			♣			♣
40		♣		△⊗		△
30	♣	△⊗	△⊗		♣	⊗
20	△⊗				♥⊗△	♥
10	♥	♥	♥	♥		
0	Fathers	Mothers	Sr. men leaders	Sr. women leaders	Black men	Black women

♥ Excluded, ⊗ Pressured to work, △ Burned out, ♣ Exhausted

women leaders were highest on stress because they took on the most responsibility for supporting employees during the pandemic in addition to family responsibilities. It is not the first time women emerged as the care factor in organizations. This should be of concern because women are leaving the workforce in large numbers (Lean In, 2020). Even if they stay they are less likely to rise into senior positions than men. Who will be the care factor when they are gone?

In another study, nearly 70% of the C-level executives across from the United States, United Kingdom, Canada, and Australia are seriously considering quitting for a less stressful job. Yet, almost half of workers believed their executives did not understand how difficult the pandemic was for them (Hatfield et al., 2022; Kelly, 2022).

Why was it that workers did not know that executives understood the stress everyone was undergoing? Leadership missed the opportunity to show empathy and reveal they too were human. I have seen this lack of personalization during other times of stressful change such as mergers or business transformations, executives leave the communication to impersonal emails and videos.

While the McKinsey study covered a specific time period it has implications regarding who is most impacted by large scale changes. As we struggle to recover from the fallout, the temptation is to increase demands on training and implementing new initiatives that will place more pressure on managers and support personnel. This will not work long-term. The need is to simplify. Cut back on bureaucracy, make time for human interaction that leads to trust and open communication.

Investing in mental health is as important as keeping the machinery going

We need to change our attitude towards mental health. If we considered people just like a valuable machine on the factory floor, we would find and treat the root cause. In a factory, if the line kept shutting down or putting out low quality product we would investigate what was causing the malfunction. In the workplace when we see stressed workers, increased conflict, absenteeism, people with psychological injuries and a high attrition rate, rarely do we investigate the root cause or treat it.

Every employee deserves support. I've been on the other side of recommending that an employer let an employee go because they represent a potential danger to others. Employers often seem frightened that they don't have enough to sack an employee , yet they are oblivious to the exposure of not taking action.

Companies need to tackle difficult workplace conversations early. And employees need to be able to report that they need more support to do their role and trust that there will be positive action. Otherwise people will learn there is no reward for being honest and vulnerable and will choose to resign.

Melissa Matthews, mediator, family dispute
resolution practitioner

I have seen similar comments on surveys where people expressed frustration at having reported bullies and for abuse, but they did not see any action taken. The HR response is that legally they cannot reveal any disciplinary actions they might have taken. This explanation seems hollow when the person reported continues to behave in the same manner. These are difficult issues to resolve and indicate that we need a different perspective on how to follow up on these incidents. Perhaps there needs to be ongoing support for the victim.

Employers can help by providing resources like mental health days and online therapy sessions. But middle managers should regularly check in with workers and foster an environment where workers feel comfortable asking for help or letting someone know when they are overwhelmed. This can be difficult because the stigmas associated with mental health and addiction can keep workers from seeking help.

The transition to remote work makes it even more important for managers to check in on employees' mental health. Without the ability to walk around and talk casually with employees, virtual conversations can slip into only discussing work. If they cannot do it on team calls managers will have to schedule time with people to ask how they're doing.

It will take strategic approaches from multiple disciplines to recover from this crisis. All entail alignment with the human side of organization to be successful. But as usual the answers can be found by asking and conversing with members of your workforce. This is a survey comment that may serve as an example of the wisdom hidden in your workforce.

Prior to Covid, mental health was still a stigma in society. Post Covid, it really has been brought to light what everyone is going through. I would like a program developed for mental health. Perhaps a certain allotment of hours provided to each employee when a mental health day is needed (almost like sick time). Our job is high stress and the expectation to come in day in and day out is tough. Those tough days that are tougher than others, it would be nice to take a mental day break to recharge that brain that often times needs to be recharged. It would allow said employee to hit the reset button and return to work next day ready to tackle the day.

Office worker in utilities

Emotional culture of compassion lowers burnout

Hidden in the academic concepts of emotional intelligence is an ancient truth. Emotional maturity grows with the insight that the heart plays a much larger role in communication than the mind. The question then becomes how to grow our hearts?

Dare we use the word love instead of emotional intelligence? Vietnamese Zen Buddhist monk, teacher, and peace activist Thich Nhat Hanh teaches the idea that "understanding is love's other name." That to love another means to fully understand and empathize with their suffering. "Suffering" refers to any source of profound dissatisfaction—physical, psycho-emotional or spiritual. In *How to Love* he writes,

> When we feed and support our own happiness, we are nourishing our ability to love. That's why to love means to learn the art of nourishing our happiness. Understanding someone's suffering is the best gift you can give another person. Understanding is love's other name. If you don't understand, you can't love.
>
> Thich Nhat Hanh

Understanding others begins with self-compassion. When we are hard on others it is because we consciously or unconsciously fear we will be held responsible for their error. Expanding our hearts through self-compassion enables us to let go of the fear and extend it to another. If you feel this is all too fluffy for the workplace, ponder how you feel when you are completely accepted and feel you belong. This feeling isn't often available and yet it is generated by simple acts like saying thank you or how can I help with that?

What I have derived from this advice is that first is self-care. Given the stressful conditions that we are facing this becomes critical. We all play a very important role in the success of the organization even though we may not feel it all the time. Caring for ourselves and others will help everyone succeed.

Barsade (2014) refers to an "emotional culture that consists of the emotions employees do and should express at work." They called it an *emotional culture of compassion and love*. He found that when employees were able to express caring, compassion and affection it was correlated with lower burnout/stress levels.

Their findings were based on a study of nursing homes where they measured tenderness, compassion, affection and caring. They did not ask participants if they felt or expressed those emotions themselves, the researchers asked to what degree people saw their colleagues expressing them.

They also measured employee withdrawal and their levels of emotional exhaustion by studying their rates of absenteeism. They found that units with higher levels of compassionate love had lower levels of absenteeism and employee burnout. It also showed up in higher levels of employee engagement through employee satisfaction surveys. Barsade states,

> The view that dominated our field for 20 years was that anytime you engage in emotional labor — meaning you're changing or regulating your emotions for a wage –that's going to lead to burnout, What we're suggesting is that it's more complicated than that. It may well be that even if you don't start out feeling the culture of love — even if you're just enacting it — it can lead to these positive outcomes.

Using the words *compassion* and *love* in the workplace may be increasingly acceptable as spirituality emerges as a diversity topic at work. This trend is appearing because more employers are concerned about creating more fulfilling and culturally inclusive work environments. These needs seem to be a driving force for developing new products, improving customer service, and creating other business or organizational values. Spirituality is also emerging as a topic that empowers individuals in the workplace to challenge and change systems of oppression (Byrd, 2018).

Note

1 Occupational Health and Safety Management—Psychological Health and Safety At Work—Guidelines For Managing Psychosocial Risk.

Bibliography

American psychological assoc. (2021). Health crisis pressures psychologist workforce. *Survey of Psychologists*. Accessed June 14, 2022. https://www.apa.org/pubs/reports/practitioner/Covid-19-2021

Barsade, S. (2014). Why fostering a culture of compassionate love in the workplace matters. *Knowledge at Wharton Staff*. Accessed May 12, 2022. https://knowledge.wharton.upenn.edu/article/fostering-culture-compassion-workplace-matters/

Byrd, M. Y. (2018). Spirituality and diversity in the workforce. In *Diversity in the workforce*. Routledge: New York.

Canadian Occupational Safety. (2021). Psychological injury claims on the rise. Accessed July 21, 2022. https://www.thesafetymag.com/ca/topics/psychological-safety/psychological-injury-claims-on-the-rise/312494#:~:text=The%20Workers'%20Safety%20and%20Compensation,%2C%E2%80%9D%20according%20to%20the%20report

Chaney, M. P., & Hawley, L. (2018). Developing human resource development competencies to manage sexual orientation and transgender, Chapter 7. In M. Y. Byrd, & C. L. Scott (Eds.), *Diversity in the workforce*, pp. 120–153. Routledge: New York.

Clark, T. (2020). *The four stages of psychological safety. Defining the path to inclusion and innovation*. Berrett-Koehler Publishers: San Francisco, CA.

Daniels, I. D. (2021). *Hermeneutic phenomenological study of the lived experience of black workers' exposure to psychosocial hazards in the American workplace*. Capitol

Technology University. Accessed July 11, 2022. https://www.proquest.com/docview/2626931391?pq-origsite=gscholar&fromopenview=true

Eisenberger, N. I., Lieberman, M. D., & Williams, K. D. (2003). Does rejection hurt? An FMRI study of social exclusion. *Science, 302*, 290–292.

Fani, N., Carter, S. E., Harnett, N. G., Ressler, K. J., & Bradley, B. (2021). Association of racial discrimination with neural response to threat in black women in the US exposed to trauma. *JAMA Psychiatry, 78*(9), 1005–1012.

Hatfield, S., Fisher, J., & Silvergate, P. G. (2022). C-Suite's role in wellbeing. *Deloitt.* Accessed July 1, 2022. https://www2.deloitte.com/us/en/insights/topics/leadership/employee-wellness-in-the-corporate-workplace.html?id=us:2sm:3li:4diUS175466:5awa::MMDDYY::author&pkid=1008950

Hutchingson, G. B. (2022). Private mental health practioner. *LinkedIn Post.* Accessed May 10, 2022. https://www.linkedin.com/posts/jennifermcnelly_activity-6929406751020646400-Q7HD?utm_source=linkedin_share&utm_medium=member_desktop_web

Indeed. (2021). How to prioritize inclusion and belonging in a hybrid work environment. https://in.indeed.com/insights/inclusion-and-belonging-in-hybrid-workplace?hl=en&co=IN

Islam, Z., Ganga, S. A., Mohanan, P., Rahmat, Z. S., Chbib, D. E., Marfani, W. B., & Essar, M. Y. (2021). Mental health impacts of Lebanon's economic crisis on healthcare workers amidst COVID-19. The national library of medicine. Exist June 14, 2022. https://www.ncbi.nlm.nih.gov/pmc/articles/PMC8652701/

Kelly, O.C.G. (2022). The looming threat of boss loss: Most senior leaders plan to join the Great Resignation, Global Survey Finds. https://www.kellyservices.com/global/about-us/news-center/news-releases/ocg/2022/the-looming-threat-of-boss-loss-most-senior-leaders-plan-to-join-the-great-resignation-global-survey-finds/

Lean In. (2020). Women in the workplace. Accessed May 12, 2022. https://womenintheworkplace.com/

Lloyd, C. (2021). One in four black workers report discrimination at work. Accessed August 16, 2022. https://news.gallup.com/poll/328394/one-four-black-workers-report-discrimiiok87unation-work.aspx

Lloyd-Jones, B., Bass, L., & Gaëtane, J. (2018). *Gender and diversity in the workforce. Diversity in the workforce.* Rutledge: New York.

Mandavilli, A. (2018). The world's worst industrial disaster is still unfolding. *The Atlantic.* Retrieved July 27, 2022. https://www.theatlantic.com/science/archive/2018/07/the-worlds-worst-industrial-disaster-is-still-unfolding/560726/

Masten, C. L., Eisenberger, N. I., Pfeifer, J. H., & Dapretto, M. (2013). Neural responses to witnessing peer rejection after being socially excluded: fMRI as a window into adolescents' emotional processing. *Developmental Science, 16*, 743–759.

McKinsey & LeanIn.org. (2020). Women in the workplace. Accessed May 5, 2022. https://www.mckinsey.com/featured-insights/diversity-and-inclusion/women-in-the-workplace

Mental health impacts of Lebanon's economic crisis on healthcare workers amidst Covid-19. The national library of medicine. Accessed June 14, 2022. https://www.ncbi.nlm.nih.gov/pmc/articles/PMC8652701/

Microsoft work trend index. (2021). Accessed March 1, 2022. https://www.microsoft.com/en-us/worklab/work-trend-index/hybrid-work

Microsoft Worklab. (2021). The next great disruption is hybrid work – are we ready? Accessed May 27, 2022. https://www.microsoft.com/en-us/worklab/work-trend-index/hybrid-work

Pandley, E. (2021). Mental health is the next big workplace issue. *Axios.* Accessed July 30, 2022. https://www.axios.com/2021/08/16/mental-health-is-the-next-big-workplace-issue team

Parker, S. K., Knight, C., & Keller, A. (2020). Remote managers are having trust issues. *Harvard Business Review.* Accessed August 29, 2022. https://hbr.org.

Saad, L., & Wigert, B. (2021). Remote work persisting and trending permanent. https://news.gallup.com/poll/355907/remote-work-persisting-trending-permanent.aspx

Shannon, C. E., Rospenda, K. M., Richman, J. A., & Minich, L. M. (2009). Race, racial discrimination, and the risk of work related illness, injury, or assault colon findings from a national study. *Journal of Occupational and Environmental Medicine, 51*(4), 441–448.

Slack. (2021). The great executive – employee disconnect. Accessed April 22, 2022. https://slack.com/blog/news/the-great-executive-employee-disconnect

The Conference Board. (2021). Accessed August 1, 2022. https://www.conference-board.org/press/Return-to-Work-Survey-June2021?isid=enterprisehub_us&ikw=enterprisehub_us_lead%2Finclusion-and-belonging-in-hybrid-workplace_textlink_https%3A%2F%2Fconference-board.org%2Fpress%2FReturn-to-Work-Survey-June2021

The Guardian. (2022). Millions face a second pandemic of mental health issues. *The Guardian.* Accessed June 14, 2022. https://www.ncbi.nlm.nih.gov/pmc/articles/PMC8652701/

Weick, K., & Sutcliffe, K. (2009). *Managing the unexpected.* Jossey-Bass: San Francisco, CA.

Welcome Trust.org. (2022). Accessed June 14, 2022. https://wellcome.org/

WHO. (2021). Accessed July 21, 2022. https://www.who.int/news/item/16-09-2021-who-ilo-almost-2-million-people-die-from-work-related-causes-each-year

Worksafe Australia. (2022). Psychosocial hazards contributing to work related stress. Accessed July 21, 2022. https://www.worksafe.vic.gov.au/psychosocial-hazards-contributing-work-related-stress

Yang, L., Holtz, D., & Jaffe, S. (2022). The effects of remote work on collaboration among information workers. *Nature Human Behaviour, 6*(1), 43–54.

5 The secret life of human social systems

- Human/Social systems frameworks for emotions and feelings
- The light and the dark side of social identity
- Socializing humanity into technology
- Measurements for social systems

For thousands of years medical practices were held back because humans couldn't see and didn't understand the microbes that were making us ill. Today, our organizations are held back when managers don't see or understand the psycho emotional factors that affect organizational behavior. Few corporations have actually made a systematic effort to design their methods of governance in congruence with human nature.

There is hope that exposure to these factors will encourage managers to look beyond "hard facts" to solve relational problems. Hard science didn't solve Covid-19 because it couldn't change people.

An inadequate understanding of social systems is one of the reasons leaders are not able to detect the early signs of impending tragedies like the Macondo well explosion and Chernobyl meltdown. It is possible that the technology problems are now understood and can be avoided. But the social, political and communication norms will probably repeat themselves so that the next tragedy will also find culture and leadership as root causes.

The ability to understand the meaning of the way people interact in conversations and their mannerisms provides risk management data in the form of psycho emotional clues. For example, those who knew the Transocean Offshore Installation Manager on the BP oil rig knew his mannerisms well enough to know he was very stressed about going forward with the well completion and the transition to production. But the communication norms only supported speaking up about technical concerns. People reported his stress as an indicator that something was wrong after the fact but at the time it was not recognized as a red flag.

So the goal of this chapter is to inform leaders, managers and others exposed to high-risk situations that the human social system is designed to provide information to help us survive. Sometimes it comes verbally in the form of an engineer or worker that raises a concern. Other times it is unspoken and

DOI: 10.4324/9781003368724-5

transmits itself as an emotion or feeling. Unfortunately emotions are typically dismissed as "noise." This deprives managers of valuable data to prevent failure. As Scharmer and Pomeroy (2019) commented,

> Traditional science relies almost exclusively on one form of knowing—that of the mind and, second, its methodologies are designed to examine what *is* in that moment. *Progress, however, is usually driven by the ability to sense what is ready to emerge.*

Those signs typically come from subtle signs of stress or discomfort.

Why do we dismiss feelings? There is no sense in blaming managers and supervisors for the slip ups in the human social systems. Very few were taught how to work with people. It is time to acknowledge that leadership development begins at the psycho dynamics level. That takes some deep work because acknowledging that emotions and feelings are part of the work processes means having less control and managers are expected to be in control. Equipment and engineering are one thing but controlling others' emotions, feelings or conversations is out of the question.

Our understanding of the connection between human social systems and organizational performance has increased exponentially since 1997 (Zohar, 2000). Showing concern for employees increases the willingness of employees to adopt company practices (Gittell, 2009; Gittell et al., 2006; Nonaka & Takeuchi, 1995). Informing and training is not enough. There is a higher acceptance that it is the social contracts that generate high performance (Gittell, 2009; Rozovsky, 2015).

So we begin with learning some basics about the influence of human systems on organizational performance. First through the lens of complexity science and then through power relations, which both constrain and drive the system. Next, we proceed to some of the basic concepts that help explain why people do what they do, how we impact each other and finally, how technology and the human system interact.

Complexity insights transformed our understanding of social human systems

Complexity management involves the study of social interactions at multiple levels and their effects on organizational adaptive and emergent outcomes. Ralph Stacey and Dave Snowden have been developing new ways to make sense of human interaction and human systems. Stacey refers to human systems as complex responsive systems and Snowden refers to Anthro-complexity (Snowden, 2016). They both maintain that human complex systems are different from natural, biological or technical complex systems. That would be because the interacting elements are human beings, who are in themselves complex adaptive systems.

In my estimation one of the most important contributions that Stacey and colleagues have made is their view of conversation as *complex responsive processes* (CRP). Each conversation or interaction we have produces a reaction that can potentially change the direction of an event, a relationship or an organizational strategy (Stacey et al., 2002). This view of conversation has consequences, which will be covered in Chapter 6, for the way we plan change initiatives and related communications.

CRP increases uncertainty in human systems making predictability scarce. This changes the manager's role from designer and observer to active participant, not controller. In fact, what goes on in the field or plant floor may have little to do with management influence unless they are present or have developed relationships with those involved.

People decide on the truth in interaction with each other

Rasmussen, a safety scientist, built on these ideas about social human systems and conversation. Concerned with accident prevention he introduced the concept of *boundaries of safe operation*. This concept could be of use to other disciplines to explain why employees don't always follow procedure. Engineers can provide specifications to operate equipment safely. But in the field unexpected risks emerge and employees make decisions all the time about how to address them. They know how close they can come to the limits of safe boundaries before the equipment fails. Rasmussen suggested not to try to control for error through tighter procedures. He recommended giving the information needed to prevent failure and how to make decisions using it to the individuals doing the work. But we still face the dilemma of how to motivate people to follow a process.

What you will read next may sound like brainwashing, but it is the way culture forms. Talcott Parsons (1991), one of the most influential sociologists, was particularly interested in how adults were included or excluded in work groups. His theories present a very concrete way of understanding the effect of human social systems on individual and organizational performance.

When business leaders say they want to have a culture of safety, they are saying they want to socialize employees to follow the safety and health protocols. But, the culture already has unspoken rules that you must follow to be a part of the group. They may or may not include following safety protocols. When people do follow the rules it is because they know that if they don't they cannot be team members in good standing.

Parsons analogized this quality of the human system to a biological system's ability to produce and maintain itself by creating its own parts. He wrote that human social systems generate and regenerate the norms of what is acceptable through human interaction—repetitive, recurring communication. An example is how Instagram and Twitter shape public opinion.

What this means is that the work group defines what is the correct way to do a job and re-enforces it via impromptu recurring conversations that spread quickly. In contrast, traditional business communications are slow and infrequent. Parsons was saying that employees needed to be socialized to follow protocols and that it would only happen through persistent interaction. This should make managers reconsider the amount of administrative work they give supervisors because it takes time away from the important work of interacting with employees. They need to be with employees to influence their sense of identity and belonging

Identity and belonging

Social identity theory is one of the most powerful concepts to understand inclusion and exclusion. Social identity and personal identity are two ways that people see themselves. To ignore either of them would make trust and communication difficult. Social identity is the part of the Self defined by the groups that we belong to. It describes the conditions under which social identity becomes more important than one's identity as an individual (Tajfel et al., 1979). That is why exclusion from the group feels like a personal loss.

The loss of a social identity can be a devastating loss or a liberation. Historians point to the conscription of African Americans into the Civil War by the northern Army. It was a huge advantage for the North but the South was faced by a dilemma. Blacks could not be conscripted into the army because that would make them humans, equal to other soldiers. That change in social identity would have brought the construct of slavery into collapse.

Today we are still fighting for women to get equal pay because the old social identity of the man being the breadwinner is still in play. These two examples demonstrate that social identities are tied to power. Each time a significant social identity shifts, someone has less power or views themselves as having less. That dynamic is that the heart of why DEIB is a difficult transformation.

Belonging is tied to social identity: a set of shared beliefs or ideals. To feel a sense of belonging, you must feel unity and a shared understanding with and among members of your group. This helps us to understand why most diversity programs fail. An outsider will not feel they belong just because you are friendly and invite them to join the group. No matter good intentions, without shared understanding the sense of belonging with each other cannot exist. It takes patience, skilled listening and the ability to ask questions to get to the heart of a person. Then you might find common ground.

Personal identity is how you see yourself as a unique individual. These are your interests, talents, values, likes and dislikes and your goals. It is often referred to as your self-image. The strength of our personal identity helps us know who we are and have confidence. It can also be the source of suffering when we compare ourselves to others or we do not meet a standard. When this happens there is a voice in our head criticizing us for failing. Or perhaps we are angry at a person or group that we feel rejected us. The persistence of these thoughts leads to mental health problems. We are talking about this now because there are ways to prevent that.

For example, let's say we receive feedback that we often don't listen. We've worked hard on our listening and pride ourselves on it. One way to deal with the inner critic is to let our pride take over, refuse the feedback and withdraw. Another way is to use our cognitive abilities to release the negative emotions and evaluate the feedback with an open mind.

Sometimes feedback can help us grow, but we cannot know that unless we are able to go to the source and ask questions. One of the hallmarks of an inclusive leader is the ability to separate personal identity from our value as a human being. Some would call it letting go of our ego. That allows for listening with an open mind to find a way back to common ground. Sometimes this is possible and sometimes it is not.

Power and status are always a part of belonging and inclusion

Complexity management often refers to the influence of power in all human relating. No one can do whatever they want, because we are all subject to the pressures of those higher up and the from peers. Much of the conversation about psychological safety is an attempt to mitigate the uneven balance of power so that people can speak up with their concerns or disagreements. But it doesn't seem to work often.

Power is related to status. Both are strong elements of the social system that drive decision-making in organizations. Those with more power can allocate resources to achieve their ends without regards to the impact on other parts of the organization. Yet regulatory agencies largely blame disasters on poor culture and leadership. In his book, normal accidents, Perrow (1984), said the poor engineering that caused the Ford Pinto auto fires had nothing to do with culture. They did not happen due to values, beliefs or artifacts. It happened because of the desire for profit and the power of individuals.

Whether Perrow is correct that the desire for profit and the power of individuals is separate from culture does not matter. What matters is that neither the government nor the people seem to be able to change this imbalance.

There are examples that lack of attention to human needs does not serve long-term benefits. Status inequality in work roles can cause mistrust, which leads to poor performance. For example, when pilots feel more important than baggage handlers. Gittell (2005) investigated the perils of these power dynamics. She interviewed employees from Southwest, American and United airlines. She found there were significant differences in the way employees regarded each other. At United and American there was a hierarchy where pilots were at the top and baggage handlers were at the bottom. Each group had their job assignments and would not pitch in to help any other group.

At Southwest it was very different. Employees spoke well of each other and pilots would help to clean the cabin when necessary. Gittell et al. (2006) tie the quality of relationships to each airline's stock price after 9/11. While most airline share prices stayed down, Southwest recovered 92% of its share price within four years while United's shares were still at 12% of their pre 9/11 price.

Empowerment as a substitute for inclusion

Although Southwest has long been envied for their financial success, not many companies are able to replicate their culture. Even though why they are successful is not a secret, the norm at other airlines is to treat people as strategic resources, human capital.

Empowerment is an attempt to balance the status and power between management and workers. Unspoken is the knowledge that this empowerment can be taken away at any time. It is line management that decides to whom and when to grant autonomy. This type of empowerment is not about sharing power. It is human capital management and employees can sense that it is not real.

False promises of empowerment have made employee engagement difficult because all too often employees have learned that what is good for the company is not necessarily good for them (Batt & Appelbaum, 2013; Cushen, 2013).

Empowerment obscures power differentials but you cannot get rid of the difference. It exists in every system. Employees know and accept this reality. Building relationships between those with power and those without power could be seen as a manipulation to avoid resistance. And it can be.

The same may be said for the diversity and inclusion initiatives. Building inclusive relationships after people have lost trust in a company or in a manager would be difficult. But can be done. Recognizing that all human beings deserve respect and an equal opportunity to fulfill their physical and emotional needs provides a fair and solid basis for collaboration.

Managing culturally diverse social identities

In the United States, race is a life-altering category, but in a country like China, for example, ethnicity and nationality are much more salient to how people see themselves and others. Many countries outside of the English-speaking world don't have a concept of race that is similar to that in the US, or they don't have a concept of race at all. It's important to be aware that people may not consider themselves members of the social group you might ascribe to them.

When managing a culturally diverse group creating a common social identity is challenging. When a group first comes together they are all operating from a different place of belonging. Bringing them together into a team takes intentional work.

One of the simplest and best-established strategies to decrease bias is to create activities for people from different social identity groups to get acquainted. Consider which social identity groups do not often interact and arrange opportunities for connection. That may be working together on a project, organizing a social event, bringing people together for a retreat or team-building activity.

Equity may be an issue in multicultural settings if certain ethnic groups are treated as subservient to others. It might also exist in any organization when the culture supports a *high power distance*. Even in cultures with *low power distance* employees typically do not bring up their boss's mistakes for fear of consequences. Yet bosses feel quite free to tell employees about their mistakes. Even in a culture where that is acceptable, it can create feelings of inequity.

Equity is one of the most difficult social needs to meet. It is about giving people access to the resources they need to succeed. It is not about equality because one person may need more flexibility in their work schedule while others are required to follow a set schedule. Something to consider when creating a new policy; examine how it may impact people with different combinations of social identities. Pay special attention to social identities that may be underrepresented or oppressed. How would it impact people of color? English as a second language speakers? Single mothers? Disabled folks?

When making the decisions about who can work from home consider the equity questions. The people working from home will save on gas and car maintenance. If it seems like the policy could create a burden on certain groups, consider how you could adjust it and be sure to check with people who have social identities likely to be impacted.

Darkside of social identity

It turns out that social identity may be the source of all human conflict. Social identity can help thin and fit people feel good about themselves, but it leads to prejudice and discrimination against people who aren't thin and/or fit enough to belong to the group.

When we feel insulted what is reacting within us? It is our reaction to the threat of losing our social identity. The mind is socially conditioned to believe that if you want to have status, you have to belong to a group. The reliance on the collective group for fulfillment can lead to actions that go against personal values as was demonstrated by the Asch (1951) experiments where individuals knowingly answered questions wrong just to give the same answer as the rest of the group. They did not know that the rest of the group was instructed to give the wrong answer to test the experimental subject. Not being different becomes more important than asserting personal convictions.

There is status associated with social identity. The question is whether rank is ever fully separable from the more innocent concerns surrounding daily relationships. I don't believe it is, which means that social identity is not innocent. It can be instead a kind of shackle. Our social identity restrains us from within and cultural biases confine us from without. To belong we must fit in and the culture determines where we can fit in.

After several tremendously tragic high school shootings in the U.S., it made me think even more about social identity. High School groups self-form through joining with those who are the most similar to them. Evolutionarily there is still some part of us that feels safest when we are with people who are like us. The group provides protection and resources to the individuals and the group as a whole. Anyone who does not belong is not afforded the same protection. The shooter is always an outcast who may belong to a fringe group but is usually alone and angry. So they set out to get even and destroy the sense of security that they envy.

It is not unusual to find an employee survey comment that reflects feelings of being treated like an outcast. In my experience because it is usually a lone voice, it is ignored. There is an unwritten agreement that if several people do not express a sentiment, it can be safely disregarded. But isn't it the lone outcast that becomes the shooter or lights the forest fire. Perhaps even one statement expressing pain and suffering deserves more than a passing glance.

What a conundrum. Social identity helps us to know where we belong. It can also isolate, and contribute to conflict. Breaking through silos, prejudices, and "outsider" status is all about piercing social identity. This challenge is central to any change effort. It can be done. Snowden points out that humans do not simply respond to stimuli; we can make choices. We can also substantially alter the world around us to suit our purposes. We can also move between roles depending on context and have the ability to realign our social identities (Snowden, 2016).

Social fields

When people who have a shared identity come together it is called a social field. The social field concept is helpful because it makes it easier to understand how human beings affect each other without words, even if they do not know each other. It is a way of understanding the invisible dynamics that affect our behaviors and decisions. Social fields are formed and controlled through social interactions, specifically the conversations that take place between members of a group. So if you want to influence the nature of these conversations and behaviors, you and your direct reports must be involved in the group's social field.

Another example of social fields is professional identities. Design engineers might form boundaries to become efficient and to separate themselves from the environment (Luhmann, 1984). This is necessary to maintain group identity and regulate behavior. Members continuously work to maintain their separate identities (Luhmann, 1997). This is where the barriers to collaboration across functions lie.

A supervisor and their team are a social field. The qualities of the field determine how well the team performs. At a manufacturing plant a group of supervisors were discussing a lack of accountability around safety. They said that one of the reasons it was lacking was that they were unable to discipline anyone. Then they told the story that one supervisor had their windshield shattered after he issued a safety citation. After that there was only one supervisor (Rob) who would discipline members of his team.

Even talking among themselves they recognized that the relationship that Rob had with his team was very different than the relationships they had with their team. One of them said, "Rob, they respect you. If my people were more like yours I wouldn't have the same problems."

Rob nodded. "You've got to take the time to talk with them. I make a point of speaking with each of my team members to find out how things are going and if they needed anything."

And that's why Rob's team was different from the other teams. He had created a social field where people felt included and respected. As he demonstrated, the best way to do that is to reach out and have personal conversations. That does not mean that the supervisor has to be friends with everyone or that there will never be conflict. The point is to make people feel they can bring up concerns and have things addressed in a timely manner.

Emotion is the language of the human system

Emotions shape the social system and matter in every aspect of human endeavor (Van Kleef, 2009). They, "…are a constant and necessary aspect of human existence. They infuse the actions, behaviors, thoughts, feelings and decisions made by actors (Conner, 2007: 16)." We cannot make any decision without them because ultimately we rely on that gut feeling to make a choice. This fact was discovered when surgery deprived a patient of access to their emotions (Damasio, 1999).

So you would think emotions would be taken seriously in the workplace. But they are not because most of us are taught to leave our emotions at the door. Of course, this isn't possible so we have to hide them. This brings about all kinds of problems. For example, instead of talking about mistrust and anger to resolve differences, they store up and block communication. This leads to not sharing information that could prevent the next failure. Unfortunately emotions are typically dismissed as signs of immaturity or weakness.

Even though the emotional state of employees affects their ability to perform, supervisors receive little education on how to approach the topic. For example, many studies in the healthcare industry link social emotional and higher cognitive skills to the quality of patient care. Measuring the emotional climate can be a real-time indicator of patient safety and highlights the importance of emotion as a precursor to safe or unsafe care.

These studies also found that more accurate and faster diagnoses were made with neutral or likable patients than those labeled negative. Physicians and nurses felt sad, fatigued and angry when working with patients who displayed anger or mental health problems. This led to the staff spending less time on taking their history, examination and treatment (Heyhoe, 2013; Heyhoe & Lawton, 2020).

Exposure to rudeness and incivility also hurts performance. The opposite is also true. Physicians spoke about a sense of collaboration created by colleagues sharing concerns about diagnostic uncertainty. Showing vulnerability often increases confidence in a plan to gather more information or pursue a treatment. It makes sense that not being able to share uncertainties left doctors feeling isolated, and this decreased their awareness of potential threats to patient safety.

Emotions are contagious, even more so when people are within the same social field (Hatfield et al., 1994). The actions of the leader affects those closest to them and those feelings are passed on to others. How far it goes depends on the force of the impact. One example with enormous consequences was how the CEOs of the major airlines reacted after 9/11.

The airline industry was devastated. Huge layoffs took place with major airlines such as American and United. Southwest airlines stood out as an exception. The CEO decided that layoffs were not an option. Southwest Airlines CEO Jim Parker "indicated a willingness to suffer these immediate losses in order to protect relational reserves and maintain longer term performance" (Gittell et al., 2006: 317).

The emotional impact of those decisions was quantifiable. After 9/11 a study of US airlines found a strong correlation between meeting the socio-emotional needs of employees and financial sustainability.

The stock prices of airlines that did not lay off personnel were at 92% of their pre-9/11 level within four years following the attacks. Whereas, the ones that did lay off people were at 12% after four years. The airlines (Delta and Southwest) that did well on stock price also scored higher in productivity, union relations, and lower in conflictual relationships.

Emotion is the language of the human system. If you ignore emotions you don't know what's going on and are susceptible to all manner of unwanted consequences.

You can only influence change from within the social field

Explaining the influence of the social field Böll, a biologist researching complex human social systems said, "How I show up influences how you feel and how you feel influences how I can show up (2018)." We are a dynamic field of needs, attitudes, sentiments, emotions, expectations and perceptions impacting each other. Our decisions and actions are not independent acts. They are influenced by the voices of our teachers, parents, peers, and experts present in our mind consciously or unconsciously.

Organizational change takes place at the level of interpersonal interaction between leader and follower. If the leader is not present, it ends the intended process. Too often the change management plan includes intensive communication campaigns with senior leaders holding community forums, and then dies off if another pressing issue takes their attention. Worse it is often impersonal and there is very little follow-up regarding the issues that emerge from the dialogues. Consequently, employees are left directionless. The following comment about a failed Lean initiative is a good example.

> One of the biggest issues I have encountered is when executive leadership says all the right things (and I believe truly means it) but middle management isn't on board. When your manager (or worse THEIR manager) is the problem, employees become disengaged because they get mixed messages and have nowhere to turn for clarity. The larger the company, the more likely this will happen. And the harder it is to get access to somebody at a high enough level to address the situation.
>
> (Nuclear engineer, USA)

Continuous communication is the lifeblood of any initiative. Senior leaders cannot be expected to communicate personally with hundreds or thousands of people. Their direct reports and then those that report to them down to front-line leaders need to be inspired and in constant communication to implement the plan. However, senior leaders are ultimately responsible for how and what is communicated. The consultant or team lead managing the Lean transformation can't be blamed if employees see the initiative as an excuse to get rid of their jobs. That failure lies in the hands of senior leadership for not providing support or guidance. Most people are not aware that priorities and expectations are communicated.

Priorities and expectations are communicated moment to moment through social interaction. In the social field it is the way we treat each other, the way we relate, think and act that creates how we feel about our work and how well we do it.

Relationships in the social field make neural connections (us) smarter

Dan Siegel, interpersonal neurobiology researcher, writes about social fields, "Simply said, human connections shape neural connections, and each contributes to the mind. Relationships and neural linkages together shape the mind (2012: 3)." The outcome is similarities in socio emotional development and how members of the field think and feel. "Even engineering design, which is traditionally thought of as a strictly technical process is a social process of interaction and negotiation between participants, who bring their knowledge and awareness of the object being designed" (Cross, 2011: 20).

Within the social field thoughts and feelings are contagious. Any communication coming from outside the field fades by comparison. That is why a manager, team leader or teacher can create a high-performing social field regardless of leadership in other parts of the organization. The popular movie *Stand and Deliver* is a true story about a teacher in a low-income Mexican American neighborhood. He alone believed that there were students there who could learn calculus and pass the advanced placement exam. He created the social field for them to learn and they all passed. The folks that administer those tests did not believe the results so they took it again under observation and passed again.

There is a lot more proof that these fields exist and it is known how to create them. It is all available in the research on GSFs (Böll, 2018).

Generative social fields

Now that you know a little about social fields you're ready to understand why some of them are generative while others are degenerative. The GSFs Initiative is a collective effort to deepen our understanding of how we impact others and how they impact us; and how shifts in these relationships can lead to the transformation of individuals, families, and organizations.

A social field naturally exists when a group of people gather for a common task or purpose. A conscious and unconscious connection forms that permits the experience of shared emotions. In a GSF the shared feelings of acceptance, belonging and security allow for learning and collective creativity that yield beneficial outcomes (Scharmer, 2016; Böll, 2018; Senge et al., 2015).

The research on GSF's comes mostly from educational settings. One of their characteristics is that they make it safe to fail and share knowledge (Böll & Senge, 2017). This is vital, especially for adults, because the fear of failure is anxiety tied to learning.

A GSF is a way for us to come to understand how the individual's personal system shows up with other systems—including other human beings. A personal system includes the physical, such as the cardiovascular system, and it includes the emotional system. In other words when you approach people or work with them you are aware of them as a total person. They are not simply students or hired help.

When training individuals to generate GSFs the first area covered is emotional awareness. Emotions are rarely experienced consciously. They are reactions that turn into feelings. And those feelings cause us to react. A clenched gut is an indication that something is amiss. The mind might interpret it into a feeling of fear or excitement. An emotionally aware person notices that and can make a conscious decision to act or not to act on it.

For example, studies show that it takes about 30 seconds to decide if you want to have anything to do with someone when you first meet. Becoming more self aware and inclusive is only possible if we can extend those 30 seconds into longer time periods before making judgments.

The more intentional we are about how we show up, the more control we have over the quality of the social field. The person with authority has the most influence so teachers cannot blame the student and managers cannot blame the worker for the condition of the social field.

If you attempt to change things with the same mindset, nothing will change. Our way of being is the only agent of change. The way we create GSFs is to show up as a supportive leader who believes that every employee is capable and wants to contribute to the success of the organization. Excellence follows when the right resources are in place. For a school it would be skilled teaching, quality curriculum, supplies and facilities. For a work team it means clear expectations, priorities, resources, personal development and clarity of purpose.

A simple way of thinking about the extraordinary performance of some work teams is how a great sports team is deeply grounded on self-awareness and collective awareness. What can I do and what does the team need? As Peter Senge says, it's a paradox. "It is all about me and it's not about me at all." How I show up as a manager is important. But it isn't all about me. It's about my impact on the collective social space.

Earlier you read about teachers like Tom Hall who guided Black students from the ghetto to extraordinary academic accomplishments. I've heard many people refer to these results as magical because they cannot understand how these results happen. Now you know.

What is the relationship between human and technical systems?

The relationship between humans and technical systems is at risk because it is not fully understood. LearnSafe, a European-funded project to study organizational learning, collected data from over 1,000 participants. In both the nuclear and oil & gas industries the barriers uncovered were both technical and social. In the social system, leadership was often a root cause of accidents. On the technical side were limited resources, conflicting priorities, difficulties with formal system and procedures. They warned that the focus should not be on social and technical systems individually, but on the interactions among them.

In spite of the evidence, approaches to organizational improvement continue to focus on the technical first and sometimes address the social issues without understanding. Here are some comments from practitioners and researchers on this topic:

> Human performance people go technical first then try to bring in the human factor. We are lacking understanding of how relationships work to sustain an intervention. The norm in high risk environments is to talk the technical and when things get challenging we are going to have to address the interpersonal, but it is distasteful. We need to normalize those interactions and socio tech. Start with personal interactions. If you build systems based on the values that people bring, buy-in follows.
>
> (James Marinus, 2020)

> The truth is that there are no concepts or ideas within safety science that fully address social structures (at least not operationally within industry). In fact, there is still work to be done to validate theoretical positions and conceptual frameworks that are grounded in operational reality.
>
> (Clinton Horn, 2020)

For example, management tends to address the people side of organizations by controlling human error, incentives, posters, behavior observations, cardinal rules and awareness programs (Levenson, 2011; Loud, 2012). These activities may help prevent errors that can be somewhat predicted by cause-and-effect thinking. They do not address the complex social system problems such as sharing information or listening to divergent points of view. This is not surprising since engineers tend to be more comfortable with design and technology than sociology.

What is missing is attention to social needs such as the need for equity, belonging and inclusion. It is a paradigm shift to accept that the technical problems may not be solved if the social needs are not met. The reason is that, "…at the core of organizational longevity is the interaction of social, emotional and cooperative whole human beings in various kinds of personal relationships to each other" (Schein & Schein, 2018).

Technical skills and knowledge cover what you need to know about the work performed by your team or organization. For example, as a college president, you need to understand financial management and fundraising. If you manage a group of safety engineers, you need to have a good grasp of safety engineering. You need to know enough to ask questions, make good decisions, set intelligent priorities, and offer useful guidance. Understanding the value of conversations and inclusion can help foster trust, communication and collaboration. These are the coveted "soft skills" that enable high performance.

Sociotechnical systems

Emery (1959) and Trist (1978), were socio psychologists that were the first to write about sociotechnical systems. They worked with the coal miners in the 1950s one of the things they discovered was that prior to mechanization the miners had been able to organize their work and schedules to meet production and individual needs. Mechanization destroyed their social network. Each person worked individually on a repetitive tasks to be more efficient. The result was disastrous. People stopped taking care of each other, illness and injuries increased and production went down.

It was a very clear lesson that still goes unlearned. We redesign our organizations without considering how it will affect the relationships. We introduce new technology with insufficient socialization. In 2020 PG&E pulled the plug on a $300 million Accenture change effort because people did not buy into the new IT systems. One company decided to use unassigned cubicles for employees working from home and at the office. The immediate reaction was anger because now they were not allowed to bring in any personal photos or make the cubicles personal in any way. Whoever planned that change did not understand human social needs.

It is likely that managers focus on the technical systems because human issues are so complex. One such change taking place now is the hybrid workplace. Almost eight in ten people say they want to continue to work from home more often than they did before Covid-19. The challenge is maintaining relationships when people no longer see each other on a consistent basis. Supervisors and managers will need excellent sociotechnical skills.

Sociotech theory of joint optimization

The sociotechnical system theory is founded on two principles. One is that success or failure results from the interaction of social and technical organizational subsystems. The second is that the socio does not behave like the technical, people are not machines. With growing complexity and interdependence the technical can also start to exhibit nonlinear behavior.

It explains why and how human social systems interact with technical systems to drive performance. Both systems must be optimized to work with each other. Otherwise you will have a great social system, and a great technical system that are in conflict. The boundaries of safe and productive operations have less to do with technical specifications than they do with social expectations. Sociotechnical theory, therefore, is all about "joint optimization"—adjusting the technology to human needs and providing people with the skills and knowledge to use the technology successfully.

Figure 4, Joint Optimization of Sociotechnical Systems, illustrates some of the elements in the social system that need to support the technical systems for optimal performance. Trist and Emery coined the phrase, *joint optimization*.

The Chernobyl nuclear power plant tragedy is an example of social factors outweighing the technical. The investigation uncovered that people who lacked technical understanding of the technology made flawed decisions leading to the disaster. Information regarding flaws in the system were hidden from the managers operating the plant so that Russia could meet its nuclear power goals (Kapitza, 1992). Based on the belief that reactor technology was inherently safe and that there was a technological fix for most problems, Soviet planners opted for premature selection and early fabrication of the reactors. Their cost-cutting measures resulted in reducing their margins for error (Josephson, 1991).

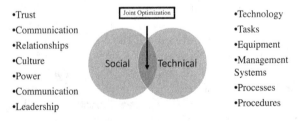

Figure 4 Joint optimization of sociotechnical systems.

In the aftermath of the 1986 Chernobyl disaster, most of the lessons being learned were about the technical, radiological, environmental, and medical consequences of that event. Although these aspects are significant, broader social and psychological factors greatly contributed to the catastrophe. These cultural issues were the fundamental cause of the Chernobyl accident.

Socializing technology

Leadership is a social art that capacitates technology. Cameron Stevens (2022), a safety advisor, is one of the most knowledgeable and ardent proponents on the primacy of technology in safety. It began when he realized rising in the organization did not improve his influence on the safety of work. "There was more influence on design as you often had a big role in crafting strategy, however, ultimately tech drove most of the change in work practices (along with political pressures, commodity prices etc.)."

Technology has more influence because it has shifted work practices. An example is how virtual video communication has changed communication patterns. The safety profession should learn from this, he says, because most safety people still rely on improving procedures or leadership training to advance safety. But, improved understanding of the role that technology plays in shaping the design, experience and safety of work is critical to achieving better results.

I got two insights from listening to Stevens. First, even though he is saying that technology is driving change, he is also saying that the change is not possible without the proper *mindflex*. Second, as he listed examples of how technology is helpful he also said that it does not eliminate the human side of safety. For him, "Technology is an enabler. The role of technology when implemented in an ethical, responsible and sustainable manner is to elevate the role of the human. To enable human flourishing."

Here are a few examples. Artificial intelligence can provide risk insights that as humans we do not have the cognitive resources to identify. A drone can go into a confined space but you still have the human elements to deal with. A safety management system can collect information digitally but using the information is a human issue. For example, a face mask with responsive technology makes it easier for a person to use a checklist, but it does not necessarily insure acting in accordance with it. A checklist, just like a behavioral observation form, is only as helpful as the individual's belief in its usefulness. He adds that, "We really should be starting with the checklist first before we even start to consider digitizing."

In Stevens' experience when he introduces the opportunities that technology presents, about 50% of the safety advisors begin to talk about all the drawbacks. This reaction is an outcome of the field's tendency to focus on what could go wrong, rather than highlight the potential to improve the design, experience and safety of work. I tend to agree because I have had the same experience when introducing social intervention such as relationship-building and conversational communications.

S&H professionals focus on finding things that are wrong because that is how they are educated. Even the hiring practices try to weed out personalities that don't follow the rules exactly. The goal is to select people who are less likely to have accidents. What you are really doing is weeding out people who are open to change and innovation. However, as Stevens said the successful use of technology only comes with a mindset that enables innovation and change.

Stevens often talks about the social acceptance of technology in our daily lives. That our personal tech social norms are a key metric for the likelihood of accepting the same digital technologies in the workplace. For example, if you use a smartphone at home to send a video of two different dining tables at IKEA to choose from to give visual context, then you are far more likely to send videos of two different pump configurations in the planning phase of a complex pipework installation job when you are at work.

Stevens admits that it took a significant traumatic experience for him to change his mindset. It involved the birth of his daughter. He realized while she was an infant that all he saw was danger around her. He lost sight of the exciting adventure she was on when she explored the house. With the help of a psychotherapist he was able to realize that the limitations he was setting for his daughter could limit her ability to deal with uncertainty and the unknown. He went on to look for other opportunities in the S&H industry to work full-time with technology. In two months his mental health had significantly improved. His story is one more example of the stress involved with the S&H profession. Always looking for risk and to prevent failures it's very taxing.

Stevens' comments also illustrate just how important it is to address employee mindsets with the introduction of technology. Doing that takes more time than we probably think we need and more conversations. The 73% failure rate of digital transformations frequently reported suggests that slowing down to socialize the technology first saves both time and money in the end.

He concluded by sharing his prediction that, "The future belongs to S&H advisors who have the necessary mindset and skillset to drive the adoption of emerging technologies in their organizations. Co-designing and implementing a human-centered safety-tech strategy is the greatest opportunity to improve S&H this decade.

How do you measure results in the social system?

"The real is relational," wrote Bourdieu (1992: 97), one of the foremost authorities on social fields. There is so much meaning in this sentence. It can be interpreted as the relationship between parts in a system or as the human dynamic of coming to agreement on what is true in relationship with others. The challenge of measuring in the social field is how to prove interrelations if there is no agreed upon cause and effect? How do we observe the invisible?

Social and cognitive psychologists believe emotions and feelings can be precursors to accidents. However, social phenomena are hard to quantify. This may lead to dismissing it as invalid data. Weick (1995) reminds us that people's emotions and feelings have an effect on perception and behavior, and that their influence on organizational and safety performance should not be dismissed, even if they cannot be quantified.

One of the ways to measure performance is by measuring employee perceptions. There is ample evidence provided by studies over the years that relationships, the way people perceive they are treated, and their relationship with their boss correlate to an organization's level of performance (Gallup Q12, 2020). Positive answers to questions like "I have confidence in the leaders at my company or "Leaders at my company demonstrate that people are important to the company's success" are associated with high-performing organizations that practice diversity and inclusion (Culture amp, 2019).

It would seem that hurtful emotions develop into negative organizational outcomes. While these measurements are important, measurement is not the same as explanation. When dealing with the complexity of social interaction numbers will not suffice. Could those responsible for the survival of the organization let go of the belief that numbers are what keeps them from falling into the abyss?

For now, corporations are more conscious of maintaining a pulse on employee perceptions and mental wellness through qualitative surveys. It remains to be seen what happens with the data. The problem I've observed is that anything relational is messy and complex. Managers are not trained to deal with people dynamics and those who are do not have the authority to change what needs to be changed. Those folks might be in organizational development, human resources, health services, employee assistance or other helping professions.

Are measurements in the social system helpful?

Deming stressed the importance of data so why would he say, "It is wrong to suppose that if you can't measure it, you can't manage it... a costly myth (Carsten, 2019)." There are many things that cannot be measured but must still be managed and decisions must be made about them. Particularly in dealing with people, change is constant. Just because something happened in a certain way once, does not mean it will happen that way again. So a manager is forced to decide how much to rely on measured data.

During a LinkedIn dialogue Carsten Busch added that what you measure is what you get. "Often measures misdirect resources either because they invite gaming the measure, or because it triggers interventionism. Especially when the measure has become the goal." The goal to improve S&H gets lost in meeting the dashboard metrics. Another practitioner expressed frustration at a different problem with metrics, "There is an un-willingness to accept that we can improve – all of our indicators are either Green or 100%, so how can there be anything to improve?

Elisa Lynch, safety advisor, talked about the stress measurements can cause, taking energy from making people safer (2020).

> I can't overstate the stress and anxiety that can be caused by the measurement of these often meaningless stats. I have vivid memories of panic ensuing anytime an injury occurred – first thought would be "hope he's OK" followed shamefully quickly by "the TRIFR is gonna go to sh*t and god help you if it occurred at the beginning of a project, where you don't have the man hours to absorb the statistical impact, the graph shooting up so vertically that it's gone off the page, never to return to the earth's surface again.
>
> And so then the "injury management" would begin, the manipulation of RWI vs LTI vs MTI, the phone calls, the mounting pressure – Should the medical cert really say that? No capacity?? Take him back to the doctor! Get him on light duties!! All in the name of safety and targets
>
> Whenever someone drops the quote "what gets measured gets managed", my mind automatically thinks, "what gets measured gets manipulated..."

The point is that when it comes to the human social systems, we can't rely on quantitative goals. For example, tracking documented mandatory conversations usually ends up in the same place as behavioral observations. Either one usually gets pencil-whipped. As one supervisor told me, "We both just sign the sheet and say we talked. It is a waste of time."

Nevertheless most people will say, I will believe it when I see it. Show me the change. How do you know if trust has increased other than asking people in anonymous survey? You can observe people treating each other in a more respectful way and sharing information. Also because emotions are contagious most people can feel a difference in the environment. Linking back to business results can be done through correlation with absenteeism and reduced accidents. But those are lagging indicators and it is not a cause-and-effect relationship. Inclusive leaders do not need numbers to believe that trusting people and treating them respectfully will improve performance. But the company demands metrics so we must have them. Hopefully, however, now that you are learning about how your social systems are operating you will have other ways of knowing the emotional state of the organization.

If you are going to measure, then measure what goes right

Measuring what goes right can be challenging but you learn so much more by doing that. As Noriah and Beer (2000) commented after 40 years of working with change in organizations, "The organization's ability to learn from its experiences is a legitimate yardstick of corporate success."

Hollnagel (2014) has a refreshing take on measurement. He uses the concept of Safety II, which defines safety management as a tool to ensure that 'as much as possible goes right, which means that safety is managed by achievements and, consequently, is measured by counting the number of cases where things go right, not merely by the number of failures. Of course, this approach does not mean that traditional measures are unnecessary, but they are considered a part of safety management, not a measure of success.

Human social systems view of organizations

In this chapter, I presented a view of organizations as human social systems. The traditional perspective concerns itself with structures, processes, and efficiency. Social is all about people, their psychological needs and their interactions. The social systems perspective underscores that behavior is shaped more by the group than the individual. For example:

- Building relationships and networks is foundational to success on any project.
- When organizational change involves the people impacted they are more likely to support it.
- It is easier to do something when peers are doing it too. So when you need to change something, change it with a group. The more people are involved, the more likely it is that others will follow.
- Emotions and beliefs spread throughout the social field. When a few people complain about something, everyone soon starts complaining about that thing. The reverse is also true; model different behavior with a few people and see how it spreads.
- How people interact carries more weight than individual actions. So interact in a way that allows every voice to be included. Spend time together to build PS between people.
- Resistance is a psychological and social process. Lowering anxiety lowers resistance.
- There is no such thing as hiring the best people. People will perform in line with PS, feeling heard and respected. Don't keep toxic employees, no matter how good they are.

Bibliography

Asch, S. E. (1951). Effects of group pressure upon the modification and distortion of judgment. In: H. Guetzkow (Ed.), *Groups, leadership and men*, pp. 177–190. Carnegie Press: Lancaster.

Batt, R. L. and Appelbaum, E. (2013). The impact of financialization on management and employment outcomes, Upjohn Institute working paper; 13–191. DOI 10.17848/wp13-191

Böll, M. M. (2018). Introduction to the Meeting. In *Brochure for the first gathering in generative social fields*, October 1–3, 2018. Garrison, NY. https://bornslivskundskab.dk/wp-content/uploads/2019/10/Agenda_Generative_social_field_color_print_simple.pdf

Böll, M. M., & Senge, P. (2017). *Compassionate systems.* MIT J-WEL. Accessed May 2, 2020. https://jwel.mit.edu/assets/video/compassionate-systems

Carsten, B. (2019). *If you can't measure it…Maybe you shouldn't: Reflections on measuring safety, indicator, and goals.* Self-published: MindtheRisk.com (pp. 27–29).

Carsten, B. (2020). LinkedIn dialogue.

Conner, J. (2007). *The sociology of loyalty.* Springer: New York.

Cross, N. (2011). *Design thinking: Understanding how designers think and work.* Berg Publishers: Oxford.

Culture amp. (2019). 2019 diversity and inclusion report. Accessed July 23, 2022. https://cdn2.hubspot.net/hubfs/516278/2019_Diversity_and_Inclusion.pdf

Cushen, J. (2013). Financialization in the workplace: Hegemonic narratives, performative interventions and the angry knowledge worker. *Accounting, Organizations and Society,* Volume 38, Issue 4, 314–331.

Damasio, A. (1999). *The feeling of what happens: Body and emotion in the making of consciousness.* Harcourt.amasio: New York and London.

Emery, F. (1959). Characteristics of socio-technical systems. Reprinted in Emery, F. 1978, *The emergence of a new paradigm of work.* Centre for Continuing Education, Australian National University: Canberra. https://www.thirdstage-consulting.com/digital-transformation-gone-wrong-at-pge/

Gallup Q12. (2020). The relationship between engagement at work and organizational outcomes. *Meta Analysis.* Accessed May 12, 2022. https://www.gallup.com/workplace/321725/gallup-q12-meta-analysis-report.aspx

Gittell, J., Cameron, K., Lim, S., & Rivas, V. (2006). Relationships, layoffs, and organizational resilience: Airline industry responses to September 11. *The Journal of Applied Behavior Science, 42*(3), 300–303.

Gittell, J. H. (2005). *The Southwest Airlines way: Using the power of relationships to achieve high performance.* McGraw-Hill: New York.

Gittell, J. H. (2009). *High performance healthcare: Using the power of relationships to achieve quality, efficiency and resilience.* McGraw-Hill: New York.

Hatfield, E., Caccioppo, J. T., & Rapson, R. L. (1994). *Emotional contagion: Studies in emotion and social interaction.* Cambridge University Press: New York. Accessed May 9, 2020. http://www.lessicom.it/wp-content/uploads/2011/12/Emotional-contagion1.pdf

Heyhoe, J. (2013). Affective and cognitive influences on decision making in healthcare. PHD thesis. University of Leeds: Leeds.

Heyhoe, J., & Lawton, R. (2020). Social emotion and patient safety: An important and understudied intersection. Accessed May 4, 2020. https://qualitysafety.bmj.com/content/qhc/early/2020/03/25/bmjqs-2019-010795.full.pdf

Hollnagel, E. (2014). *Safety–I and safety–II. The past and the future of safety management.* Ashgate: Farnham.

Horn, C. (2020). Safety and health consultant comment on LinkedIn.

Jones, B., & Cox, S. J. (2005). Facilitators and hinderances to learning within the UK nuclear sector. In Organisational knowledge and learning capabilities (Proceedings of the 6th European Conference Boston).

Josephson, P. R. (1991). Atomic culture in the USSR: After and before Chernobyl. In A. Jones, W. D. Connor, & D. E. Powell (Eds.), *Soviet social problems.* Rutledge: New York (pp. 55–77).

Kapitza, S. P. (1992). Lessons of Chernobyl-the cultural causes of the meltdown. *Foreign Affairs, 72,* 7.

Levenson, N. (2011). *Engineering a safer world: Systems thinking applied to safety.* MIT Press: Cambridge, MA.

Loud, J. (2012 March). Taking safety seriously: A contrarian view of the safety practice. *Professional Safety, 57*(3), 55–61.

Luhmann, N. (1984). Social Systems. (J. Bednarz & D. Baecker Trans). Stanford, CA: Stanford University Press.

Luhmann, N. (1997). Theory, culture & society. Sage. 14(1): 41–57.

Lynch, E. (2020). LinkedIn Post 8/11/2020. https://www.linkedin.com/posts/elisalynch_ep-35-what-is-the-relationship-between-leading-activity-6699043652351619072-lzu7

Marinus, J. (2020). Operations consultant comment on LinkedIn.

Mearns, K., & Yule, S. (2009). The role of national culture in determining safety performance: Challenges for the global oil and gas industry. *Safety Science, 47,* 777–785.

Milgram, S. (1974). The perils of obedience. *Harper's Magazine.* Archived from the original on December 16, 2010.

Nohria, N., & Beer, M. (2000). Cracking the code of change. *Harvard Business Review.* https://hbr.org/2000/05/cracking-the-code-of-change.

Nonaka, I., & Takeuchi, H. (1995). The knowledge creating company. Knowledge Management Metazine.

Parsons, T. (1991). *Social system.* Routledge: London (p. 138).

Perrow, C. (1984). *Normal accidents: Living with high-risk technologies.* Basic Books: New York.

Rozovsky, J. (2015). Five keys to a successful team. Accessed November 6, 2018. https://rework.withgoogle.com/blog/five-keys-to-a-successful-google-team/For

Scharmer, O., & Pomeroy, E. (2019). Social field residence: How to research deep structures of the social system. *Field of the Future Blog.* Accessed August 17, 2022. https://medium.com/presencing-institute-blog/social-field-resonance-how-to-research-deep-structures-of-the-social-system-544d68654abf

Scharmer, O. C. (2016). One earth, two social fields. *Huff Post.* Accessed May 10, 2020. https://www.huffpost.com/entry/one-earth-two-social-fields_b_578e922de4b-0f529aa0746fb?guccounter=1&guce_referrer=aHR0cHM6Ly93d3cuZ29vZ2x-lLmNvbS8&guce_referrer_sig=AQAAAKkAQ4dWDOFtt7bgdIroj5u1Bu5sp-gKYBYHmeVSO9bgEhSpVYxK5DE6xklBzJaSJDfnnB_xELFBU3H9auI8H-HELim8HnhKqkBsVjqVJvpSNkByVn2sbKvG_-RsHNhg3jC1ibEtpmG6wbxx-fT5XBFdwV4ACU05MVYx4z2wozTyK_o

Schein, E. H., & Schein, P. A. (2018). *Humble leadership: The power of relationships, openness and trust.* Berrett-Koehler Publishers: San Francisco, CA.

Senge, P., Scharmer, O., & Böll, M. (2015). Towards a lexicon for investigating generative social fields. A report prepared for the Mind-Life Institute Academy for Contemplative and Ethical Leadership.

Siegel, D. (2012). *The developing mind: How relationships and the brain interact to shape who we are.* Guilford Publications: New York. Accessed May 29, 2020. https://www.drdansiegel.com/pdf/Chapter%20excerpt%20from%20TDM%202nd%20Ed. pdf

Snowden, D. (2016). *Three or five.* The Cynefin Company. Accessed July 26, 2022. https://thecynefin.co/three-or-five/

Stacey, R. D., Griffin, D., & Shaw, P. (2002). *Complexity and management: Fad or radical challenge to systems thinking?* Routledge: New York.

Stevens, C. (2022). Personal conversation with Rosa A. Carrillo.

Tajfel, H., Turner, J. C., Austin, W. G., & Worchel, S. (1979). An integrative theory of intergroup conflict. In W. G. Austin & S. Worchel (Eds.), *Organizational identity: A reader*. Brooks and Cole: Monterey, CA. (pp. 56–65).

Trist, E. L. (1978). On socio-technical systems. In W. A. Pasmore & J. J. Sherwood (Eds.), *Sociotechnical systems: A sourcebook*. University Associates: San Diego, CA.

Twaronite, K. (2019). Five findings on the importance of belonging. *EY*. Accessed May 11, 2022. https://www.ey.com/en_us/diversity-inclusiveness/ey-belonging-barometer-workplace-study

Van Kleef, G. A. (2009). How emotions regulate social life: The emotions as social information EASI model. *Current Directions in Psychological Science, 18*(3), 184–188.

Weick, K. (1995). *Sensemaking in organizations*. Sage Publications: Thousand Oaks, CA.

Zohar, D. (2000). A group-level model of safety climate: Testing the effect of group climate on microaccidents in manufacturing jobs. *Journal of Applied Psychology, 85*(4), 587–596.

6 People-centered change management

- Properties and realities of change management
- Why most communication plans fail and how to succeed
- Change involves learning and learning involves change

Traditional change management models assess the present, identify the vision, then plan how to close the gap between the current and preferred reality. The emphasis is on planning, defining roles, processes and procedures to direct decision-making and behavior. Then managers are expected to have the skills to implement said plan without diverting from it.

Neuroscience and complexity principles are redefining the transformational change process. For instance townhalls, videos with senior executives explaining the reason for change and written materials are still part of the communications mix. But the emphasis is on conversations in one on one and small groups that allow for clarification and expression of concerns. The information gathered in this way is then used to course correct the process. Conversation between all levels of management is also important for alignment because the voice of leadership is represented via team leaders, supervisors, managers or executives. Neuroscience exposed the importance of belonging, inclusion, respect and autonomy in any process involving learning or change. These were not the focus of change management models of the past.

One of the leaders in this field is Ralph Stacey (2010). His work is an unusual combination of disciplines: economics, therapy and complexity science in organizational change. For purposes of determining how to approach change in social human systems his agreement & uncertainty framework is very useful.

Change is a nonlinear process

Dwight Eisenhower once said, "Plans are useless, but planning is essential." It is the conversation during the planning or the writing of the procedure that is important. Through planning, people develop a common understanding of the potential problems and solutions. So that when confronted with the unexpected during implementation they are able to make decisions that are

DOI: 10.4324/9781003368724-6

more likely to be in concert with the collective group mind. If conversation is the key to preparing people for the unexpected, the implications are to strive to get the people doing the work involved.

Plans do not serve as predictions. Managers rarely have complete information before they must act. Trial and error dominate organizational decision-making and thus organizational change (Stacey, 1996; Wheatley, 1992). As a result the following precepts are reshaping change management theory. Everyone engaged in a common endeavor receives messages from others, transforms, and sends messages to others. As a result each agent adapts to changes in unique ways as they happen. The myriad of interactions amongst all of the participants makes surprises inevitable, some good, and some bad. In fact, control through policy and procedure may be undesirable if the prescribed solution does not fit the emergent circumstance. A better tool may be the use of natural social networks to ensure the latest information needed for good decision-making is kept updated and transmitted to key parties.

The recognition of chaos and complexity brought new ideas into change management. One of the biggest paradigm shifts is that control and order are emergent rather than hierarchical or predictable (Dooley et al., 1995; Lewin, 1992; Waldrop, 1992).

Conversation as a recurring change mechanism

One of the theories is CRP (Griffith & Stacey, 2005). CRP theory addresses the inherent limitations of simplistic linear models of control. Human interaction through conversation is an example of CRPs. The conversations and their outcomes are understood to be complex, self-organizing, emergent and evolving. Anyone who has played the game of telephone is familiar with how the message changes as it is passed from person to person. There is no sure way to control the content of the message once it is delivered, not unless there is a structure to course correct the message at regular intervals. This makes leadership involvement through conversations a key element of organizational change. Amy Edmondson observed,

> The trickiest part of organizational change is translating the big idea into the little interactions that happen hundreds or even thousands of times a day. What are team members actually saying to one another in situations both small and large, both ordinary and earth shattering?
>
> (Amy Edmondson, 2019)

Unfortunately, a 15-year longitudinal McKinsey and Co. study (2021) revealed that executives aren't very good at generating conversation even among themselves. The inclusive leadership approach and practices are designed to help fill this gap. The goal is to not only create conversations between leader and direct report. They need to happen peer to peer.

Using the complexity model a new set of assumptions define modern change management

Engagement is the new control. Informal networks and communities play critical roles in shaping the outcomes. Formal roles may not be the key roles in the process, but leaders can influence them through their participation. Social network mapping is a useful tool to see the relationships in your organization and how information travels.

Get comfortable with uncertainty. The change process is only coherent in retrospect. Assessment of the past and present state is useful as the grounding to understand the emergent self-organization of the complex interactions between agents in the system. The assessment does not predict the outcome.

Emergence beats long-term planning: Change is nonlinear and small changes can have big effects while big efforts may not make a difference. The "emergent" aspect of change means we have to be continually looking for the effects and direction of our actions. Some may be successful in unexpected ways and should be amplified, others should be stopped immediately if they have unintended consequences. It also means successful innovations may come from unexpected people.

Failure is part of learning: Look at failure as a necessary learning process. You will not get it right in advance. Develop the skills to identify it and address it early. This means normalizing speaking up and taking action. Be prepared for "failures" as they will come often. Success creates its own failure when successful management schemes lead to rigidity and failure.

Consensus is not your friend: Continuous conversations are critical to monitoring progress and adapting to changing conditions. Too often we do not seek conflicting opinions or observations. They must be a mandatory expectation. Otherwise people may not speak up. Too much similarity in thinking locks a group into unproductive patterns of behavior that block out divergent points of view. Productive conflict generates new insights, structures, and relationships that lead toward greater adaptability. See deviance as an opportunity.

The certainty & agreement framework

The Certainty & Agreement (C&A) framework is a strategic planning tool developed by Ralph Stacey (1996). Its greatest contribution is that it can shake a group out of doing the same things over and over and getting the same results. It can help to answer:

1 Do we need to change the culture or is this a process improvement effort?
2 Does this initiative need senior leadership involvement?
3 Do we have tried and true approaches that have worked in the past to solve this problem?
4 Can we use a standard seven steps model for change?
5 Have our attempts to change this failed in the past meaning we need to try something new?

There are two dimensions to Stacey's Matrix (Figure 5). The vertical dimension is the level of agreement on what the problem is and what needs to be accomplished. The horizontal dimension is the degree certainty that the group has about how to go about changing the organization to solve the problem. I added a vector representing an increased need for inclusivity to find the solution and sustain it.

How to read the matrix: vectors

Close to certainty: issues and decisions are close to certainty when a cause and effect link is identified. Based on past experience you can decide what would work best.

Far from certainty: at the end of the certainty continuum there is very little certainty about what will happen if an approach is implemented. There would be no good method to predict outcomes at this point.

Close to agreement: you are certain that you will have everyone's backing and understanding of the problem. That helps with certainty because you might find an expert to resolve the problem or at least you will all be on the same page about what you are trying to fix

Far from agreement: people are all over the map as to what the problem is and that might make it very difficult to get an agreement for how to proceed.

Close to agreement, close to certainty: this is your golden space because everyone is in agreement as to what the problem is and how to proceed. It should be an easy implementation

Far from agreement close to certainty: this is where politicking takes place. People must be convinced to come together on a common definition of the problem and then look at the possible solutions.

Far from agreement, far from certainty: this is indeed a difficult position. Not only does everyone have different view of what the problem is they have different views on how to resolve it. This is an area of great complexity frequently called chaos.

Community building: the diagonal vector represents community. The other vectors designate the level of change needed to help us think about the types of interventions we should consider to achieve transformation. The community vector represents that which will make the transformation happen and sustain it. Community means members care about everyone's collective work, colleagues, and the company's place in the world. The caring inspires passion, collaboration, and loyalty. The leader achieves this by putting the community first and applying human systems principles.

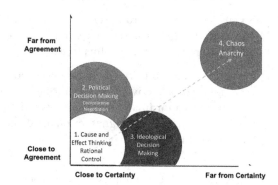

Agreement & Certainty Framework

The broken line represents community. The energy of the community fuels the transformation as uncertainty and disagreement grows in the organization.

You need more:

- Conversations
- Stakeholder involvement
- Autonomy
- Inclusion
- Acceptance of deviant ideas
- Diversity of team members

Adapted from Ralph Stacy

Figure 5 Agreement & certainty framework.

Examples of strategies that fit each area of the framework and case studies

Simple: Procedures, rules work well the closer you get to agreement and certainty. Further out within this area changing work processes may be necessary. i.e., Low quality product is above acceptable limits so "Stop the job," is instituted.

Complicated: Typically structures will need to be modified. i.e., Ergonomics, age or gender related issues, workload and supply chain issues.

Complex/Far from agreement, far from certainty: what is the right balance of working from home and on site? How do you keep people engaged? How do you make the compensation equitable for those who must travel every day to work?

Chaos: as you approach chaos there is complete lack of agreement and certainty because you are in area that is unpredictable. It is also likely that no one has been through a similar experience. i.e., In the beginning Covid-19 was a good example that. There was no certainty about proper protocols. New processes had to be set up to cover bases and at first many balls were dropped. Gradually through experimentation a solution can be found.

Applied case study 1: community

Pixar Studio has a strong sense of community. Ed Catmull, the president of Pixar, attributed the studio's success in creating a string of highly popular animated films to its

> vibrant community where talented people are loyal to one another and their collective work, everyone feels that they are part of something extraordinary, and their passion and accomplishments make the community a magnet for talented people coming out of schools or working at other places.
>
> (2008)

They have three principles. 1. Everyone must have the freedom to communicate with anyone. 2. It must be safe for anyone to offer ideas. 3. We must stay close to innovations happening in the academic community. When a company receives this type of praise, it usually recedes. "Today (2022), Pixar is one of Hollywood's most celebrated animation studios and produces some of the best and most viewed animated films."

Applied case study 2: certainty/agreement

I was working with a group that wanted workers to openly report concerns and near misses. To date they had been reporting anonymously. They had a traditional communication and training plan laid out. Then I showed them Stacey's matrix and asked, "How certain are you that you know this plan will work and that you will be able to sustain the results?" The answer was "not at all certain" because everything they had tried until now didn't work. So now the group was open to exploring different ways of approaching the solution. Without that we would have probably proceeded along the path laid out by traditional change management that doesn't work well for changing beliefs and behaviors.

Properties of organizational transformation

Attempting to move an organization toward acceptance of DEIB qualifies as a complex transformational process. Many of the processes that work were discovered through intuition which does not qualify them for scientific research but that should not rule them out. I say this because many times when executives are given "validated studies" of what works it is ignored. Nevertheless, there is guidance available for those serious about finding a way forward.

Change and interactive communication

Change happens during the moment of interactive communication between humans. Again this is why conversation is an essential aspect of managing organizational change. Ford and Ford go on to say that communication is not a tool. It is the change process (1995). But, using the word *communication* can lead us astray. The intended word is *conversation* because too often communication during change efforts is one way from management or HR communicating to employees.

I stand on 30 years of experience successfully facilitating conversations to improve communication and relationships for the purpose of improving culture and performance. Every culture assessment we've conducted to help improve performance reveals lack of communication across functions or levels of the organization.

Barriers are broken down as people have the opportunity to understand each other's perspectives. I remember a group of Mexican engineers who were surprised to learn that the American engineers cared so much about their families. The Americans were surprised to learn that the Mexicans found their emails offensive because they were impersonal and never bothered to say hello. Those insights led to improving relationships on both sides.

Executive level involvement

A McKinsey and Co. 15-year study (2021) of transformational efforts found that certain practices yield better results than others. The title of the report is telling, *Losing on Day One*. They are telling us that we are approaching these efforts in the wrong way right from the start.

Looking at Figure 6, *Losing from day one*, the most frequently used practice for all participants was setting business objectives and setting targets. The dark markers represent companies with the most successful change efforts. The column on the right indicates how much an activity increased the likelihood of successful transformation. For example, the most effective activity appears to be *executive-level weekly briefings* because companies that did that were twice as likely to succeed.

But only about 30% of the companies that responded had weekly briefings. Much more popular were the linear, tangible actions such as setting measurable goals while avoiding more difficult leadership activities such as regular conversations to align and participate in sensemaking. Successful companies also participated much more frequently on setting clear direction (targets, planning). These findings are in alignment with other researchers. But no one has quite figured out why senior executives don't act on this data.

In my experience they do not do it for two reasons, at least. One is the fact that most managers and executives are not knowledgeable about the social human systems and their impact on performance. Therefore it is not a top priority. Second, they have too many fires burning at the same time to focus any significant amount of time on one of them.

Organizations with successful transformations are more likely than others to embed transformation disciplines into "business as usual" processes.

McKinsey and Co. (2021) Losing from day one: Why even successful transformations fall short.

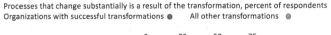

Processes that change substantially is a result of the transformation, percent of respondents
Organizations with successful transformations ●   All other transformations ○

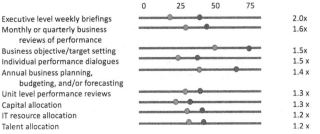

	0	25	50	75		
Executive level weekly briefings					2.0x	Increased likelihood for successful transformation
Monthly or quarterly business reviews of performance					1.6x	
Business objective/target setting					1.5x	
Individual performance dialogues					1.5 x	
Annual business planning, budgeting, and/or forecasting					1.4 x	
Unit level performance reviews					1.3 x	
Capital allocation					1.3 x	
IT resource allocation					1.2 x	
Talent allocation					1.2 x	

Figure 6 Losing from day one.

For an executive team of a large corporation meeting weekly is a huge commitment. It is not too big for a transformational initiative. But maybe too many activities are called transformations when they are simply improvement efforts. For example, it would be difficult to get the senior executives of the corporation to meet once a week about a safety culture change. Why would they? They have entire departments dedicated to safety and health. In reality, there is no difference between safety culture and organizational culture change. Anything labeled as a safety change effort is in danger of going unrecognized as a business transformation and fails to get the time and attention it needs to be successful.

Let's take an example of a successfully executed organizational transformation with a safety and health focus. Paul O'Neill of Alcoa comes to mind because he focused on safety and health in spite of all the pressure he had from the board and stockholders to put his attention on profitability. O'Neill knew that his singular focus on safety would improve the whole organization including the stock price, and it did. He is credited with saying that you can't prevent accidents unless you have an effective management system (Duhigg, 2013).

O'Neill ordered that all processes and systems be brought up to the highest standards. The way he achieved it is by demanding to be told about any injury within 24 hours. Anyone who failed to do that would be fired. And, he did actually fire someone. What that did was transform the communication system. The people closest to O'Neill had to ensure that their direct reports kept them up-to-date on any injuries and their direct return in turn also needed to be up-to-date. This went all the way down to the employee level. No one wanted to report an injury so managers and supervisors demanded that they be told of any concern so that it could be fixed before an injury took place. Now employees had the support to stop the job and get things fixed.

You can probably see why focusing on injuries ended up improving the manufacturing process, cut costs and improved efficiency. The notion of speaking up spread to all functions and disciplines. When O'neil died, a young engineer posted a tribute to him.

> I was fortunate to have joined Alcoa in 1991, just after a few years of beginning my career. After 2 months of observing the company's direction and decision-making I was struck by the money being spent on technology but without clear value to the company; so I naively (but respectfully) wrote a white-paper outlining my observations and recommendations for quantum-leap improvement to business/operations before introducing technology; sent it to Paul along with the top 30 or so senior executives, without the approval of my boss's boss. Well, what happened afterward is something I'll never forget, and what shaped my immense respect for Paul.
>
> Two weeks following my white paper, Paul sent an announcement to the entire company of sweeping changes to the top few layers of management, inverting the leadership pyramid, 24 BU Presidents, and establishing the 'Chairman's Council'; in addition announcing the quantum-leap improvement program along with an increase in BU President empowerment and accountability. This was music to my ears, but what really impressed me was Paul sending me a note, inviting me to the Corporate HQ and to shake his hand and to have lunch with a member of the Chairman's Council. Following this I was invited to join an internal group of performance improvement professionals that would go on to assist BU Presidents achieve their quantum-leap improvements. Needless to say, this was unexpected by a 29 year old "kid."
>
> Lou Pahountis (2021)

Finally, this McKinsey study raised another important find that the Alcoa story demonstrates. The companies that were successful kept the disciplines in place after the "initiative" was established. I've said this before, we can't stop doing the things that work once we've reached our goal. We can't stop having regular conversations, we can't stop thanking and recognizing people and we can't stop tending to our relationships.

What you are trying to achieve is already happening somewhere in your organization

The traditional approach to change management is analyzing the present situation, articulating a desired future state and then generating solutions to transition from where you are to where you want to be. This approach can often generate an overwhelming number of initiatives that leave people burned out. There is a faster and easier approach called *positive inquiry* and sometimes *positive deviance*.

Looking at strengths (rather than weaknesses) and what's going well (instead of what's going wrong), is a more positive, inclusive and pragmatic way of making progress. The seeds of the solution are almost always already there. All you need to do is identify them, and use them to fix your problem.

A prime example is what took place in the early 1990s (Pascale et al., 2010). Vietnam was faced with a nationwide disaster. Because of crop failure and wretched economic conditions, 65% of all children under the age of five suffered from malnutrition. The director of the American NGO, Save The Children, Jerry Sternin, was asked for help. He was given six months to make a difference and zero funding from the Vietnamese government.

Using a process he called *positive deviance*, Sternin asked the villagers if they knew of any children from poor families who were healthy. They said there were a few. When he visited, he found there were very poor families with children at a healthy weight. Sternin made lots of mealtime visits to these households to find out: "What are these successful families doing differently?"

These families collected tiny shrimps, small crabs, and snails the size of fingertips, and added these little creatures to their children's diet along with some greens. Although these elements were freely available to everyone, they were generally seen as dirty and even dangerous for young children.

They also changed meal frequency. Whereas on average the Vietnamese children were fed twice a day, these families fed their children throughout the day. This way the children could take in many calories during the day, despite their small stomachs.

Rather than run out and tell everyone he had found the solution, Sternin engaged the villagers in sharing their knowledge to educate the rest of the villagers. The program turned out to be extremely successful. Within two years more than a 1,000 children were enrolled in the nutrition sessions, and 93% of them emerged healthy. Solutions can be surprisingly low-tech, cheap and simple. Just ask yourself, where is employee engagement high? And how come? Then go learn from that group.

But wait...you've tried benchmarking and it didn't work!

Yes, the sharing of best practices doesn't always go well. Some of the topics discussed here could help us be more successful when introducing best practices from other organizations or even from within our own. For example, an Australian group did not feel the protocols developed in Montreal would work because the Montreal culture tended to be more compliant while the Australian culture prided itself on allowing autonomy.

Peer-to-peer conversations about why an approach worked and how they did it can bypass some of the resistance put up by people of different social identities. In another case a union president from an oil and gas company would travel to other O&G companies to encourage unions to buy into safety improvement efforts. His boss allowed him and a small team time off work to do that. The plant manager told me that their volunteer work kept their own safety program vital.

Be forewarned, it is not a one-time conversation. Follow up allows for course correction and dealing with the unexpected.

Change happens at the local level

The strategic planning to achieve transformation is centered on the entire organization. However, I have observed that change is going on at the local level. An H&S Director provided this example:

> I worked in a very toxic environment. There was absolutely no support from management. Getting people to follow proper procedure in dealing with hazardous waste was impossible. Trying to get them to talk to me was like beating their heads against the wall. I just wanted them to be honest with me and tell me the kinds of problems they were having with the procedures. So we started re-writing them and I would call them to ask for their recommendations. I told them that if we did not correct this problem they would be putting their families in danger. After a year I began to see a shift. When I called people they would spend more time talking with me and we had very rewarding conversations. But I will never forget the last week I was working there. I had spent five years trying to get through to one researcher. He called me to tell me that he wanted to share this information with his staff because at the end of the day he did not want them coming down with cancer because they had changed out thousands of containers without a mask. So he had transformed into one of my biggest supporters.

Too often we neglect the supervisors or the support personnel that deal with the repercussions of introducing a change effort. Fortunately, some push through on their own. For more to succeed we have to engage the local leaders by supporting them through the psychological and learning stages of change. (See *Learning and change are the same process* below).

We tend to reserve the term transformational leader for senior leaders, but they exist and we need them at every level of the organization.

Small is good

Small wins add up. A small win is a concrete, complete, implemented outcome, like increased transparency in a decision-making process such as the career development path or developing easy ways for people to book skip-level conversations with leaders.

Reay et al. (2006) conducted a longitudinal study of changing roles in healthcare. They found that creating small wins energized participants to continue the change. It might be important to avoid the usual interventions like coaching, training, or mindfulness. They reduced motivation because they raised defensiveness in response to the intervention. This is a good example of how learning anxiety can become resistance to change (Schein, 1995).

Small actions can have a larger impact than big ones. Malcolm Gladwell's book, The Tipping Point, makes this argument using epidemics and social movements as examples.

> As human beings we have a hard time with this kind of progression, because of the end result – the effect – seems far out of proportion to the cause. To appreciate the power of epidemics, we have to abandon this expectation about proportionality. We need to prepare ourselves for the possibility that sometimes big changes follow from small events, and that sometimes these changes can happen very quickly.
>
> (*Gladwell, 2000: 11*)

A 40,000 person study confirmed that tiny goals and actions were far more effective at changing behavior than ambitious programs (Fogg, 2020). You may not be disciplined enough to do a 50-minute workout, but you could do ten leg lifts or squats each time you use the bathroom. You will feel new strength in your legs quickly. His study showed that positive results are likely to motivate you to do more.

An example of a small action with huge impact is an established routine contact between leaders and direct reports. We have a lot of data on the business benefits of employee engagement, and the leadership behaviors that achieve it. For example regular check-ins via one-on-one conversations between boss and employee. Why wouldn't every CEO adopt these relationship-building practices and insist that all their managers do so?

"I don't have time" is the most frequent reason I hear for not taking the time to have relationship-building conversations. Meetings and administrative tasks take up time for managers from CEO to supervisor. While that is true, why do some leaders find the time? The ones who do take the time tell me that these conversations are the reason they get top performance from their people.

Deciding how to spend your time is a values-based decision. For some, the concept of taking time to say hello and check in on people seems against the values of hard work and focus. One supervisor told me, "Chit-chatting takes up time that should be spent on work. I don't get paid to make friends." A CEO told me, "I'm paid to make financial decisions. Let human resources take care of people."

For others, getting to know people is the key intervention to creating change. As Joe Rea, GM for 1,000 miners, tells how his region rose to #1 in safety and production.

> The shift began when I told supervisors and managers that I expected them to go out of their way to make connections with people, to say hello, make eye contact and use the employee's name each time they passed. I personally kept a list of everyone's birthday so that I could wish

him or her a happy birthday if I happened to walk past them that day. I don't go out of my way to look for people who have birthdays because if you do that for one person you have to do it for the whole workforce (1000 employees), but I make sure I chat with the ones I do come across.

(Carrillo, 2020: 69)

Many costly large-scale leadership initiatives fail. Only 25% of 1,500 senior leaders interviewed said their investment in leadership training had paid off (Beer & Schrader, 2016). According to participants even though it had been inspiring at the time, they found it impossible to apply what they had learned about teamwork and collaboration, because of a lack of strategic clarity, politics, and cross-functional conflict. "[The previous GM] had a significant impact on our organization, with all of us reflecting him in our managerial style. We are all more authoritarian than before."

Compare that to the effect of Joe Rea's story above. This simple coaching of his direct reports and follow-up transformed the morale of the organization and opened the way to implement changes that brought about substantial improvements in all aspects of organizational performance. This does not mean that all you have to do is call people by name and your organization will transform. It means that respect opens a connection to collaborate on implementing change.

Organizational improvement initiatives are relational processes

Every participant in the system is impacting every other participant, creating incredible amounts of complexity. Change happens in the here-and-now by what we do to each other and how we talk to each other. Change, good or bad, is an outcome of this reciprocal interaction. When people experience acceptance and belonging in their interactions with each other it generates the desire to contribute to the team's success. If they experience exclusion, people will disengage. So improving performance is about improving relationships

Most organizational leaders aren't aware of the relational aspects of the change process. They understand the basics about setting direction and keeping people informed but the often-heard statistics of a 70% failure rate comes from relationship failures. Change is initiated in each moment of interaction or enactment. What follows is a reaction that indicates the next step. Any change involving people is unpredictable and uncontrollable. While employee engagement and empowerment are often talked about it can threaten the power structure. So change is not the result of a mandate from the corporate office even if it comes from the CEO. It can only happen when the desired changes are enacted at the local level by engaged leaders.

An example I have in mind is typical in many manufacturing organizations. A company experiencing a high accident rate may wish to improve safety performance. However if there exists a we/they division between union or nonexempt employees and management nothing can move forward until that division is addressed.

In my experience it is not common for a leadership team to decide to address the we/they issue in a substantial manner for several reasons. One is the belief that it is quite normal for a lack of trust to exist between certain employees and managers. This is the way it's always been and it will never change. Another reason might be that past attempts have failed to change these relationships, so management has slipped into a state of resignation.

It would be a great mistake not to make it a priority to address the trust issues. Lack of trust leads to a lack of communication, which can lead to operational failure. Since you cannot improve safety performance without relationships. How exactly should they proceed to change these relationships?

Relate the change and communication to each social identity

The first thing to consider is that an organization is comprised of subcultures and coalitions with different identities, interests and goals. Sometimes they come into conflict when each group is entrenched in their own interests. That makes it hard to form relationships and trust across group boundaries.

So, to begin we must address the fundamental differences in identities between the members of different groups. It can be union versus management, maintenance versus operations or sales versus customer service. Trust doesn't happen just by putting people in the same room. There has to be a structure where individuals must work together to achieve a common goal. Additionally, they must need something from each other to complete the task.

One case involved members of an internal environmental group and the core business technology group. The tech group typically disregarded any recommendations from the environmental group. It was decided that a few members of the tech group would become part of the environmental group. The former tech members brought their insider knowledge of the core business and influential relationships with them. Then they had to learn about the environmental group. The new team was responsible for implementing a new environmental initiative. The relationships formed over time as relationships of reciprocity from regular contact during daily core work encounters.

Learning and change are the same process

Every time we learn we change and we cannot change without learning. Edgar Schein and Warren Bennis drew this conclusion from their work in T-groups at NTL (Schein & Bennis, 1965). Later, based on Kurt Lewin's work, Schein likened organizational change to the learning process. He proposed that psychological safety was an essential ingredient for successful change and learning.

Kurt Lewin's theory of psychological change posed that simply driving people to change elicits an equally strong restraining force. People do not easily give up their sense of certainty because it fulfills their need to feel safe. He identified the restraining forces as people's personal beliefs or group expectations that threaten people with expulsion if they don't meet them. "Adapting poorly or failing to meet our creative potential often looks more desirable than risking failure and loss of self-esteem in the learning process (Schein, 1995)."

Typical change management models don't treat change as a learning process. Neither do they address psychological safety. Edgar Schein and Kurt Lewin noted the emotional changes that individuals experienced as they entered a situation where personal change was required.

Schein saw resistance to change as a "learning anxiety." And, he saw psychological safety as a condition for learning. He often attempted to move people toward change by giving them new information that differs from what they knew. His research, among others, motivated Amy Edmondson's studies.

Change in the status quo triggers a state of anxiety that the unconscious may see as a threat to survival. It may be seen as a physical threat. Or it may be an emotional threat such as fear of losing control. This anxiety must be reduced to get to learning or change. Schein's point is that we often failed to consider the conscious or unconscious psychological threat that people undergo in any change process. For example, motivating a group of managers to change their management style or increase their emotional intelligence will not happen through an intellectual exercise. It is a psychosocial process that needs to consider psychological safety (Schein, 1995).

Schein's psychological stages of the change process

Whether people are asked to adopt a new technology or adapt to a new organizational design, the change process is the same. But it does vary in intensity depending on how much an individual's identity is threatened. Schein based his model on Lewin's work. Figure 7, *Psychological Stages of the Change Process,* describes five stages that can lead to the acceptance of a change.

Edgar Schein is a master at framing emotional issues into a learning context that decreases anxiety.

> It is a model upon which I have been able to build further because its fundamental concepts were anchored in empirical reality. Intellectual knowledge of the change process is not the same as the know-how or skills that are learned in actually producing change.
>
> Edgar Schein (1995)

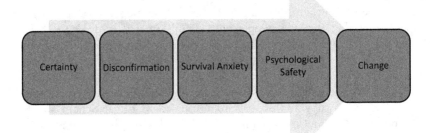

Figure 7 Psychological stages of the change process.

Certainty

Our sense of stability, according to Kurt Lewin, was created by a force field of driving and restraining forces. There were always things going on in our lives pushing us toward adaptation and they were equally strong forces holding us back from changing. It is not simple for change to occur. There are complex psychological needs for a human to function at full capacity, and change disrupts them. The idea that we can solve organizational problems by adding one more driving force such as an initiative or changing the work systems often backfires. If we don't address the fear and anxiety we will strengthen the forces against change.

Disconfirmation

"It is my belief that all forms of learning and change start with some form of dissatisfaction or frustration generated by data that disconfirm our expectations or hopes" Schein (1995).

Survival anxiety

When we accept the disconfirming data as valid and relevant, anxiety sets in. If we allow ourselves to accept change will we be admitting that we were wrong. That would mean we failed in the past. That could make us lose face, our self-esteem and maybe even our identity.

Psychological safety

Schein argued that psychological safety has to be present before disconfirming information will lead to change. In the past I have seen poor culture assessment results shared and shame those with low scores. They backfire because the anxiety raised strengthens the forces of resistance. Whenever you cause anxiety and the risk of losing face you have closed the door to communication. Consequently no change takes place.

> The key to effective change management, then, becomes the ability to balance the amount of threat produced by disconfirming data with enough psychological safety to allow the change target to accept the information, feel the survival anxiety, and become motivated to change. The true artistry of change management lies in the various kinds of tactics that change agents employ to create psychological safety.
>
> Schein (1995)

The kinds of tactics Schein refers to are forming teams so that no one person is absorbing all the responsibility; providing extra support to relieve the extra responsibilities added to the day-to-day workload; providing opportunities to practice and fail safely; and providing online coaching. These all serve the function of reducing learning anxiety and thus creating genuine motivation to learn and change.

Getting managers to even think about providing psychological safety during a change effort is a huge shift. Actually providing the support would significantly raise the success rate of change initiatives.

Lessons to consider for DEIB Initiatives

Lewin and Schein's model can apply to individuals as well as groups. The shift toward diversity and inclusion could be described within these five phases. Global power in the west rested in the hands of wealthy, educated white men for centuries. That was the status quo that powered the institution of colonialism, slavery, and the near extinction of aboriginals in the conquered lands. With the emergence of the middle class, all white men inherited a higher status than other people. That gave them and their wives to some extent a sense of *certainty*.

Disconfirmation of that secure status rains upon society daily. All disenfranchised people are rising to protest unequal treatment. The Women's March after Donald Trump's election gave rise to the wave that caused him to lose his office. The BLM and the Arab Spring movements were clear signs of a firm resolve to be treated justly. Yet, perhaps the biggest destabilizer is China's rise to super power status.

The world is certainly in a state of *anxiety*. Climate change, inflation, racism and wealth gap has made most people aware that if they do not fight for all people to have the resources to live a healthy and fulfilling life, they probably are not going to keep it for their children.

When I read this comment in a survey,

> ...operational safety, effectiveness; is at the lowest level, in my 40 years of field experience. No trust. No actions taken, at right moments. To

busy worrying about the wrong problems. No freedom to speak to each other anymore, Fear; prevails. the inclusion, and diversity, has killed the truth.

Operations supervisor (personal interview)

I realized the conversation around diversity at work has created anxiety among certain parts of the population. Someone who felt very comfortable speaking their mind is now being asked to consider how their words affect others. For some this means that their own freedom is curtailed.

Now comes the hard part, taking action that restores a sense of *psychological safety*. How do we bring everyone in the organization along so that *acceptance* of diversity and inclusion becomes the norm? Going back to Schein's comment above, "The true artistry of change management lies in the various kinds of tactics that change agents employ to create psychological safety."

The more we are exposed to different cultures, the more we accept them as normal. Movies and television shows depict the younger generation as being comfortable with people of all colors and preferences. The more I see it on the screen the less I notice the differences.

It takes a certain percent of individuals making this shift to turn it into a group or organizational transformation. Remember that emotions are contagious in a social system. Therefore, if influencers are stuck in anxiety so is the rest of their social field. So change agent, heal thyself first.

Can people grow in their acceptance of diversity

The answer is yes. People can grow in their ability to accept and thrive within social diversity. A research team examined (Ramos et al., 2019) examined 22 years of publicly available psychological, sociological, and demographic data from multiple World Values Surveys, the European Social Surveys, and the Latino Barometer. These datasets included more than 338,000 respondents interviewed in 100 countries.

> While the study focuses on religious diversity, it documents the human ability to adapt. They found that initially there was a reduction in trust of others around them in countries with increased religious diversity. After four to eight years, individuals started to report mixing with people from different backgrounds. The initial negative effect of reduced trust, was fully cancelled out by the positive effect of mixing with members of different groups. The conclusions were that people of different backgrounds and values could learn to live and collaborate together. It takes exposure over time to others who are different, patience, and opportunities to work together on mutually beneficial projects.

(Ramos et al., abstract)

Questions to assess anxiety and change readiness

Certainty

- Status quo—what is working well? What's in it for us to stay status quo?
- Feeling of control—what was under control and how was it being kept that way?

Disconfirmation

- Identifying current and potential future threats—what are the potential threats that need to be communicated?
- Who should be involved in the conversations to discuss why change is needed and how it might be accomplished

Survival anxiety

- What are the worst fears? What might fall apart if we make this change?
- How would not changing affect your job and other coworkers'?
- How would not changing affect your family?
- Are you going to be able to make the personal changes this might take?
- How likely are you to get an equal or better job if this one ends?

Psychological safety

- Request support and engagement—what type of control do you think we need to have? For example, many initiatives are implemented without concern about what is already in place and the amount of work the new initiative will create
- Form relationship network coalitions
- Develop small experiments to test change initiatives with employee input
- Have one-on-one and small group conversations to find out what's going well and what concerns need to be addressed
- Empower employees, supervisors and managers for action
- Communicate with transparency about accomplishments and setbacks
- Communicate the bigger picture for the purpose of the initiative. What is going to them or support what is already going on?

Implications for human resources

Learning is "a process that leads to change, which occurs as a result of experience and increases the potential for improved performance and future learning" (Ambrose et al., 2010: 3). Psychological safety leads to transformative learning outcomes mediated by social support, attitude toward uncertainty, and criticality. "However, the practice of human resource development (HRD) in organizations is still heavily focused on knowledge and skill delivery without allowing time and space for deep thinking and questioning: which is the essential process of transformative learning" (Nicolaides, 2020: 3).

HRD must appreciate that all changes ask every employee risk safety to test old assumptions and engage despite persistent uncertainty. The same is true of leadership development training. It takes time and preparation for a manager to become an active contributor with awareness of their deep thoughts and feelings. Short trainings have their place but retreats and longer sessions are what lead to change. It will take concerted effort to change the status quo in this area, but it must be done.

Bibliography

Beer, M., & Schrader, D. (2016). Why leader ship training fails and what to do about it. *Harvard Business Review*. Accessed July 23, 2022. https://hbr.org/2016/10/why-leadership-training-fails-and-what-to-do-about-it

Berger, J. (2013). *Contagious: Why things catch on.* Simon & Schuster: New York.

Catmull, E. (2008). How Pixar fosters collective creativity. *Harvard Business Review.* Accessed August 31, 2022. http://www.homeworkempire.com/wp-content/uploads/edd/2017/03/Reading-Material-5.pdf

Darvideo. (2021). Secrets of Pixar's animation: Why did they become so successful? Accessed September 1, 2022. https://darvideo.tv/blog/secrets-of-pixars-animation-why-it-become-so-successful/#secrets-of-pixar-s-animation-and-why-did-it-become-so-successful

Duhigg, C. (2013). The power of safety. Excerpt from the power of habit. https://static1.squarespace.com/static/5d12affb6c48770001d49960/t/5e8f7bb572793575cd328033/1586461628405/The+Power+of+Safety.pdf

Edmondson, A. (2019). https://www.psychologytoday.com/us/blog/the-fearless-organization/201906/fly-the-wall-in-fearless-organization

Fogg, B. J. (2020). *Tiny habits: The small changes that change everything.* Houghton Mifflin Harcourt Publishing Company: Boston, MA.

Ford, J. D., & Ford, L. W. (1995). The role of conversations in producing intentional change in organizations. *Academy of Management Review, 20*(3), 541–570.

Gladwell, M. (2000). *The tipping point: How little things can make a big difference.* Little Brown & Co: Boston, MA.

Griffith, D., & Stacey, R. (2005). *Complexity and the experience of leading organizations.* Routledge, Taylor & Francis: London.

McKinsey and Co. (2021). Losing from day one: Why even successful transformations fall short. https://www.mckinsey.com/business-functions/people-and-organizational-performance/our-insights/successful-transformations

Nicolaides, A. (2020). The impact of psychological safety on transformative learning: A quantitative study. *Journal of Workplace Learning, 32*(7), 533–547.

Pahountis, L. (2021). Please share your memories of Paul. https://www.pauloneill-legacy.com/your-memories-of-paul

Pascale, R. T., Sternin, J., & Sternin, M. (2010). The power of positive deviance: How unlikely innovators solve the world's toughest problems.

Ramos, M. R., Bennett, M. R., Massey, D. S., & Hewstone, M. (2019). Humans adapt to social diversity over time. *Proceedings of the National Academy of Sciences of the United States of America, 116*(25), 12244.

Reay, T., Golden-Biddle, K., & Germann, K. (2006). Legitimizing a new role: Small wins and microprocesses of change. *Academy of Management Journal, 49*(5), 977–998.

Schein, E. H. (1995a). Kurt Lewin's change theory in the field in the classroom: Notes from a model of managed learning. https://edbatista.typepad.com/files/kurt-lewins-change-theory-edgar-schein.pdf

Schein, E. H., & Bennis, W. (1965). Personal and organizational change through group methods. Wiley: New York.

Stacey, R. D. (1996). *Complexity and creativity in organizations*. Berrett-Koehler Publishers: San Francisco, CA.

Stacey, R. D. (2010). Complexity theory instituted management. https://sigs.cim.co.uk/media/2135/the_knowledgeapril2010.pdf

Stacey, R. D. (2011). *Strategic management and organisational dynamics: The challenge of complexity to ways of thinking about organizations*. Prentiss Hall: New York.

7 A critical look at psychological safety

- Why is psychological safety so popular? Is it over blown?
- Who is responsible for generating psychological safety?
- Leadership practices that promote feeling safe psychologically

The incredible popularity of the concept of psychological safety (PS) is a testament to a great need for the ideas behind it. Way before the phrase became well known people would talk about wanting to be seen and heard and how wonderful it is to be with someone who accepts you just the way we are. It is a rare feeling indeed.

In 1965 Warren Bennis and Edgar Schein wrote that a person's anxiety must be reduced before learning and personal change takes place. They called it a state of *psychological safety*. It was followed up by Khan (1990) who contributed the idea that it was also about an individual "being able to show and employ one's self without fear of negative consequences of self-image, status or career" (p. 708). He also proposed that without PS, people disengage, "withdraw and defend their personal selves" (p. 694).

But it was Amy Edmondson (1999) who popularized the concept and turned it into an attribute of high-performance teams with her 51 team study. She wrote that PS is essential to laying a foundation for effective learning and high performance in organizations. Without that, people will hesitate, or refuse, to take the interpersonal risk of speaking up, asking questions or asking for help (2002). Then in 2016 a study at Google of more than 180 teams over a period of two years duplicated her findings (Duhigg, 2016). That was when PS became the topic of the day.

There is no doubt in this author's mind about the validity of these findings. The main problem I find is that when we start using a concept over and over without understanding why it works or how to generate it, it loses meaning. It also becomes a substitute for making a real connection with employees. Employers tell employees they should feel safe to speak up if they disagree. That doesn't take the place of having a conversation with an employee who tells you about a problem and then fixing it together. And if it turns out something was your fault, thank the employee for bringing it to your attention. That is the way PS has always been generated—way before the term was born.

DOI: 10.4324/9781003368724-7

Without those conversations the concept of PS is useless. It's like when a safety catastrophe occurs and any contributing factor that cannot be adequately explained was attributed to a poor safety culture. We can now add lack of PS as a root cause. I am not sure that puts us any closer to a viable solution. But it does indicate a path because now we are talking to human interaction, the origin of culture. And we can examine how the quality of our interactions contributed to the incident.

Who is responsible for generating PS

So, who is responsible for a group's level of psychological safety. There are at least two answers to this question. First, a leader learns how to maintain a sense of PS from within. It is one of the attributes that contribute to their authenticity and ability to generate trust. The second answer is that it is a leadership responsibility to ensure the conditions for PS exist on their team or organization. This section explores the leader's responsibility to optimize the conditions that enable people to learn and change.

The pressure has mounted for executives and managers to ensure the presence of PS in their organizations. The admonitions are powerful. If they do not feel safe people will not come forward with mistakes or express their concerns, and the lack of such information could lead to substantial failures. I do agree that leadership sets the standard for PS in their organization.

The conversation is so prevalent, yet it is not common for most managers or safety advisors to receive the education they would need to become skilled in this area. So, in early 2022 I posted on LinkedIn to find out how safety advisors felt about taking on the responsibility of generating PS in the workplace. What I found was a wide range of opinions from enthusiastic embrace of PS to "There's nothing new here," "It's what we've always done," and "It's just more yada, yada." I wonder if a similar survey with line managers would produce similar results.

> I totally agree…ultimately an organisation that has better psychological safety should in turn 'theoretically' have better mental health and wellbeing but there are a number of people confusing the two concepts despite their relationship. I also view it as **not being anything new but perhaps just something that needs greater emphasis and focus.**
>
> I have no problem with the concept of "psychological safety." As I've said before, it's nothing new. The benefits for any organization wherein people feel a high degree of "psychological safety", in terms of safety, productivity, morale or otherwise, seem obvious. **My real problem is that the entire discussion doesn't seem very relevant to my reality.**
>
> **"I think a lot of safety pros don't have a psychologically safe environment themselves**, so it is difficult to think of creating/fostering that for the workers. In personal experience, I've had some success in leading

from the field level and then getting "top management" on board by that example. It's not ideal, but in the spirit of think global act local, it helps the "local" level environment.

I am investigating my last death before I retire as an OSHA investigator and I try to be a continual student in my approach and this psychological safety… **well just more Yada Yada Yada**.

If safety is a job about giving people the tools and knowledge to make safe decisions, it makes sense in an academic way to attack interpersonal or social barriers to risk awareness and mitigation. As we all know, safety professionals are in total control of all positive and negative features of a workplace culture so this makes for a great use of limited resources and credibility. **I can't think of a task most safety pros have been trained less on nor have less natural inclination to, except maybe advanced watercolors or critical analysis of French movies**.

H&S advisors are smart and not easily convinced or taken in. But, in my experience I would say it is generally accepted as a valid concept. People are afraid to speak their mind in the workplace for many reasons and we would be able to prevent more failures if people spoke up and were heard without suffering any retaliation. Unfortunately, most employees do not feel it is safe to disagree or point out errors in the workplace.

The risks of candid expression

The perceived risks of speaking your mind in the presence of people you don't trust or who have more power are very real. It seems illogical for a copilot not to alert the captain to a dangerous situation. That is until you become aware of Erving Goffman's work. He wrote about how much energy we spend hiding who we are as opposed to accepting ourselves. He observed,

> …individuals being anxious, fearful, role-playing, risk-avoiding and compulsively driven by the need to avoid embarrassment." Engaging in impression management and being in a seemingly perpetual state of cold sweat, individuals make their way through life under a tenuous social contract whose major clause is a quid pro quo (viz, I won't embarrass you as long as you don't embarrass me) premised on mutual trust and respect…" Goffman concludes, 'There is no interaction in which the participants do not take an appreciable chance of being slightly embarrassed or a slight chance of being deeply humiliated. Life may not be much of a gamble, but interaction is'.
>
> (Trevino, 2003: 14)

Leaders interested in receiving honest feedback and getting accurate information from their direct reports should take this aspect of human nature seriously. Our place in society plays a big part in how willing we are to express our thoughts as shown in the following study.

Risk escalates with loss of social status

A Culture Amp study with over 6,000 companies asked people how they felt about voicing a contrary opinion without fear of negative consequences. Figure 8 shows that all men are more comfortable expressing contrary opinions than women. Straight white men are the most comfortable. Among women, straight white women and Asian women are the most comfortable, while black women are the least comfortable expressing disagreement by a significant percent (Culture amp, 2018).

Consequently, some men may seriously underestimate how reluctant others may be to disagree or to deliver bad news. Another point of interest is that women who do voice contrary opinions, do so in spite of their fear. If someone finds themselves having to do this over and over it can become a very stressful situation (psychosocial hazard). This is of importance to leaders because it is their responsibility to be aware of these dynamics and create a situation that makes it easier for people to express their thoughts. Of course, the leader will also need to thank people when they do and consider the input even if they do not immediately agree with it.

Many books tell people how to control this fear and present their authentic self to others. The problem is that the brain is programmed with the need to belong because being alone spelled certain death to our early ancestors. As such we are sensitive to how we speak with those in higher social positions—anyone who could throw us out of the tribe. That could be our boss, someone higher up or a respected senior coworker.

Our PS sensors are quick to detect reactions that might indicate our status is at risk. Social interaction with other people is one of the biggest hazards in

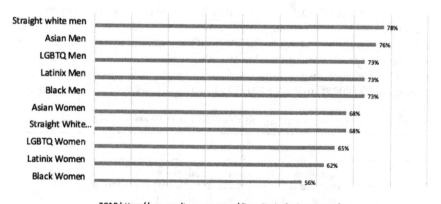

I can voice a contrary opinion without fear of negative consequences

Straight white men	78%
Asian Men	76%
LGBTQ Men	73%
Latinix Men	73%
Black Men	73%
Asian Women	68%
Straight White...	68%
LGBTQ Women	65%
Latinix Women	62%
Black Women	56%

2018 https://www.cultureamp.com/diversity-inclusion-report/

Figure 8 Voicing disagreement without fear of negative consequences.

the workplace. With each interaction we run the risk of losing face, losing credibility or offending someone important to us. It does not matter whether risk is real or imagined. What matters is that our brain functions as if it were, ever wary of saying or doing the wrong thing.

The cost of losing face

Losing face is almost a primal fear for human beings. Goffman said, "There is no interaction in which the participants do not take an appreciable chance of being slightly embarrassed or a slight chance of being deeply humiliated." He did not mean that people would necessarily humiliate others on purpose— although it does happen. Most of the time we are talking about incivilities or disrespectful comments made without conscious awareness.

An incivility is something someone says or does that makes you feel belit- tled. Most of the time they seem like small harmless actions such as somebody texting while you're trying to talk to them. Sometimes they're more serious such as receiving criticism in public. These daily events that most of us take as normal can make a big impact on morale and engagement. The *Harvard Business Review* published a 14,000 person study that was able to measure the effect of incivility on people's effectiveness at work. The results shown in Table 4 indicate that rudeness has a price tag (Porath & Pearson, 2013).

The types of incivilities included in the article were door slamming, side conversations during meetings, arriving late and keeping people waiting. The dangerous thing about these kinds of behaviors is that they are catching. People that stay working in those type of situations begin to treat others in the same way. So the cost of rudeness keeps increasing.

Fear of social interaction causes stress and shuts down communication

The Great Resignation trends confirm just how much stress is involved in workplace social interaction. Large numbers of people are quitting because they do not want to go back to the office. There are other factors such as com- muting and schedule flexibility, but the allure of face-to-face teamwork doesn't seem to be an incentive to come back to the office. Data from Slack's Future Forum Pulse (2022) survey of 10,000 knowledge workers just found that with

Table 4 Lost worktime due to incivility in the workplace

Response	Reported reaction to incivility
80%	Lost work time worrying about the incident
78%	Said that their commitment to the organization declined
63%	Lost work time avoiding the offender
66%	Said that their performance declined
48%	Intentionally decreased their work effort

a third of them back in the office five days a week, their work-related stress and anxiety reached its highest level since the survey began in 2020.

What does social risk look like from the employee perspective?

If normal social interaction is a risk, the level of risk rises exponentially when confronted with the choice to report a negative event or condition. A 2006 study came out that 58% of the nurses said they would not speak up to stop a doctor from giving the wrong medication (BMJ, 2006). They were afraid of retaliation, or even losing their jobs. This had posed a serious problem in healthcare for many years. The H&S profession also took note because it had long held the belief that the strongest safety culture was one where employees would speak up to stop unsafe conditions or unsafe acts.

It is usually very hard for managers to understand why employees feel there are negative consequences to stopping a job or reporting a mistake. As far as managers can see they have made every effort to communicate the importance of speaking up and ensured that there will not be any negative repercussions.

Comments from employees provide some light on this subject. "If I report a near miss or injury I am buried in paperwork." "My supervisor doesn't listen to me anyway." "The backlash from my supervisor makes me wish I'd never said anything. He told me that if I say anything to management it will go worse for me." The first two examples are seen as "they don't care anyway." The last one is more toxic because it generates fear in addition to resentment. Then it gets worse because the next line of reasoning is "they don't care about me." Once that happens, trust is lost and these employees stop believing they can share information with management.

If the processes that managers set up to facilitate reporting are burdensome employees will not report. Paperwork doesn't satisfy anyone's social needs—it's the opposite. If someone were to sit down with the employee and show that they listened and responded, there would be trust and open communication.

There is another factor in this scenario that shuts down communication. Employees do not believe management is in touch with what is going on in the field. "As such, even if we tell them what's wrong they don't get it." A lot of people are working long hours filling in for staff that resigned. There are resource shortages. But management response is slow. Then add that since Covid-19 the supply chain problems have raised prices on all basics. It has only made the dichotomy between labor and management bigger because upper management doesn't seem to be aware that people at the bottom of the salary range are having trouble affording basic things.

The bottom line is that asking employees to take the risk of disclosing information then not responding or worse making life harder for them strikes out several of the core needs for PS. It specifically undermines security, equity and respect.

Five core social needs for PS

These five conditions fulfill the social needs for PS. They enable personal change and learning. They lower anxiety and uncertainty, which allows the brain to absorb information faster. And ultimately, they open the way for DEIB implementation.

The most important social needs as summarized by neuro-leadership science are:

AUTONOMY: When an employee experiences a lack of control, or agency, their perception of uncertainty is also aroused, further raising stress levels. By contrast, the perception of greater autonomy increases the feeling of certainty and reduces stress (Rock, 2009).

BELONGING: Belonging is closely associated with status. Trust cannot be assumed or mandated, nor can empathy. These qualities develop only when people's brains start to recognize former strangers as friends. This requires time and repeated social interaction (Eisenberger & Lieberman, 2009). Loneliness and isolation are profoundly stressful. Cacioppo and Patrick (2008) found that loneliness is a threat response to lack of social contact, activating the same neurochemicals that flood the system when one is subjected to physical pain. Leaders who strive for inclusion and minimize situations in which people feel rejected create an environment that supports maximum performance.

SECURITY: Insecurity and uncertainty registers (in a part of the brain called the anterior cingulate cortex) as an error, gap, or tension: something that must be corrected before one can feel comfortable again. That is why people crave certainty. Not knowing what will happen next can be profoundly debilitating because it requires extra neural energy. This diminishes memory, undermines performance and disengages people from the present (Rock, 2009).

EQUITY: Studies conducted by Matthew Lieberman (2021) found that people respond more positively to being given 50 cents from a dollar split between them and another person than to receiving $8 out of a total of $25. Another study found that the experience of fairness produces reward responses in the brain like those that occur from eating chocolate.

RESPECT: The degree of respect you received from others is closely related to the groups that you belong to. Research shows that when people realize that they might compare unfavorably to someone else, the threat response kicks in, releasing cortisol and other stress-related hormones (Marmot, 2004).

PS doesn't come from on high: it is local

The behaviors and assumptions of the team leader create the conditions for PS to emerge at the local level. So what are we doing to support these local leaders in the skills and strategies to generate PS?

Corporate leaders that wish to raise the level of PS for the workforce face the same challenge they always face for any significant transformational change. It has to do with local implementation. No matter who designs the initiative or training, it is not effective until it becomes an integral part of the day-to-day work. That means that the team leaders at the front lines are the ultimate implementers.

One of the first challenges will be to raise the level of PS for those frontline leaders. Most likely they have been through an eight-hour training, or less, and left on their own to make things work. The supervisors who know how to work with people will continue to have success. Those who do not have the skills or experience will get the work done the way they always have.

A more successful route would be to build PS amongst the management ranks and introduce them to the micro-practices for inclusion. Then have them build relationships with the people that report to them. Once the front-line supervisors are responding positively they will be ready to pass it on to their teams. Continued support is essential. Feedback and sharing of information will build the confidence needed to weather the ups and downs of the experiment.

Practices for inclusion and PS

A study of 500 participants found that employees who feel included are 3× more likely to contribute to full innovation potential and 39% more likely to be engaged (Coqual, 2020). Inclusive actions fulfill the need to belong and create psychologically safe work environments for teams and work groups.

Inclusion motivates

Authentically inclusive leadership is a way of looking at how to release control while ensuring accountability. It does this by generating social interactions that support trust, learning and PS. These are the skills that will create capacity for DEIB in organizations. Generative skills go beyond knowledge of business models and professional experience to include personal development traits. Most of these practices involve conversations and relationship building, and their success is proven by substantial evidence.

Inclusive leaders create these spaces where people feel safe collaborating, creating and contributing their best ideas. Nowhere is this idea more potent than in the pursuit of preventing fatalities, illness, and serious injuries.

She turned down a 40% pay increase

I recently spoke with a Latina H&S advisor for the North American region. She had just left her past company because several people had gotten promoted, and she wondered why she has not. She talked to her boss about it and he said, "I thought you were happy with your job and loved it. I didn't know you wanted a promotion." So he promised she would have one within six months and after time had passed, she still did not have the promotion so she interviewed for another job that paid less and took it because she would learn new skills. Her boss's boss then called her and offered her a 40% increase in her salary. She turned him down, "I would rather work where someone appreciates what I do and sees my value."

Across all generations, the one-to-one check-in took priority

Fulfilling the need to belong is essential to motivating most employees to contribute and engage. The most frequently mentioned interaction with a boss that made people feel that they belonged was a one-on-one conversation that focused on helping the employee to succeed at his job. Some of the other areas most frequently mentioned were respect, being addressed by name, being heard, recognized and being thanked for specific tasks well done.

Respect status

According to the Harvard Review a recent survey by Georgetown University, respondents ranked respect as the most important leadership behavior. The research revealed two distinct types of respect. The first is owed respect, which is given equally to all members and meets the universal need to feel included. Earned respect recognizes individual employees who display valued qualities or behavior.

It also found that employees who feel respected are more grateful and loyal to their firms. The study further indicates that many employees that are new to an organization experiment with new behaviors and incorporate them when they feel that they are more respected when they act in those ways.

Call people by name

In a prison system they found that calling people by their name rather than inmate, number or miss changed behavior to be more respectful and cooperative. On a mine site with 5,000 employees, the GM asked his managers to begin looking people in the eye and call them by name whenever they passed someone. Morale, productivity and safety rose enough for the site to be recognized as a role model of high performance.

Four inclusive actions are key for leaders: (1) building trust and creating a workplace where people feel free to express themselves; (2) actively combating bias and systems of oppression; (3) embracing a variety of styles and voices inside the organization; (4) and using employees' identity-related knowledge and experiences to learn how best to accomplish the firm's core work.

Appendix A, Authentically inclusive leadership practices, provides specific actions that satisfy the five needs for PS: (1) Autonomy, (2) Certainty, (3)Status, (4) Belonging and (5) Equity.

See Appendix A for complete list of practices

Bibliography

BMJ. (2006). The wrong side of surgery: The "code of silence." 333. https://doi.org/10.1136/bmj.333.7566.484-a

Cacioppo, J. T., & Patrick, W. (2008). *Loneliness: Human nature and the need for social connection.* WW Norton and Co.: New York.

Coqual. (2020). *New study examines why belonging at work is crucial during crisis.* Center for Talent Innovation: New York.

Culture amp. (2018). *Diversity and inclusion intersectionality report.* Accessed July 22, 2022. https://www.cultureamp.com/blog/diversity-inclusion-and-intersectionality-report-2018

Duhigg, C. (2016). What Google learned from its quest to build the perfect team. *NY Times.* Accessed August 29, 2018. https://www.nytimes.com/2016/02/28/magazine/what-google-learned-from-its-quest-to-build-the-perfect-team.html

Edmondson, A. (1999). Psychological safety and learning behavior in work teams. *Administrative Science Quarterly, 44*(2), 350–383.

Eisenberger, N., & Lieberman, M. (2009). The pains and pleasures of social life. *Science, 323*(5916), 890–891: Explication of social pain and social pleasure, and the impact of fairness, status, and autonomy on brain response.

Future Forum Pulse. (2022). Return-to-office policies are hammering employee experience scores. Accessed May 12, 2022. https://futureforum.com/

Lieberman, M. (2021). https://www.uclahealth.org/news/brain-reacts-to-fairness-as-it-does-to-money-and-chocolate-study-shows

Marmot, M. (2004). *The status syndrome: How social standing affects our health and longevity.* Times Books: New York.

Porath, C., & Pearson, C. (2013). The price of incivility. *Harvard Business Review.* https://hbr.org/2013/01/the-price-of-incivility

Rock, D. (2009). Managing with the brain in mind. Accessed December 29, 2021. https://www.strategy-business.com/article/09306

Trevino, J. A. (Ed.). (2003). *Goffman's legacy.* Rowan & Littlefield: Lanham, MD. https://coqual.org/wp-content/uploads/2021/04/Power-Of-Belonging-1-Press-Release-Updated.pdf

8 Relationship strategies that improve performance

- Developing relationship competence
- The Rapid Relational Process and integration of inclusion
- The politics of managing change for improvement

Organizations spend millions to improve communication. The goal is to decrease conflict and increase alignment of purpose through the sharing of information. Overlooked is the fact that sharing information is not communication unless there is a sense of trust and shared understanding. What we want to communicate is so obvious to us that we cannot conceive of a different interpretation. We are likely to interpret another's "misinterpretation" as incompetence or worse, willful resistance.

We cannot communicate an unbiased reality. There is no objectivity. As Argyris and Schon (1974) described mental models, each of us interprets what we see according to our beliefs, conditioning and desires. We create a "reality" based on our emotional and psychological experience. Thus, divergent interpretations can start at the very beginning of a shared experience. This phenomenon is as natural as the physical laws that cause seeds to grow into trees. So, humans have limited control over their biases. That isn't something that needs changing. It needs to be noticed and managed.

The practical application of what I am describing is the secret to having an engaged workforce contributing the best of themselves. To achieve shared understanding we must first build relationship. To do that we become a source that meets the other person's physical or psychological needs. Among those needs are food, shelter, belonging, recognition, respect and autonomy. When people have those needs met, they thrive. The fruits are labor, innovation, love, art, music and more.

It is easy to accept that if we do not give a tree enough water, it will not bear fruit and probably die. But, people are supposed to grow up and provide for their own physical and social needs. An unhappy childhood is no excuse, and only the most tragic of physical injuries might merit assistance in an individualistic society. Accepting that a human being cannot perform at full capacity without having self-esteem or a sense of belonging is rare in a business environment.

DOI: 10.4324/9781003368724-8

You will note that I keep coming back to nature for metaphors. That is exactly what we are talking about now, human nature. What is the truth about human nature? Once you have decided that, you must ask, if people need respect, autonomy, appreciation and inclusion to thrive, why would we think that they will perform well without them? If we accept that people need these things, the next question would be how do we go about finding out how well we are filling those needs?

First recognize the risks of social interaction

Our psychological safety sensors are quick to detect reactions that might indicate our personal status is at risk. Social interaction with other people is one of the biggest hazards in the workplace. With each interaction we run the risk of losing face, losing credibility or offending someone important to us. It does not matter whether risk is real or imagined. What matters is that our brain functions as if it were true, ever wary of saying or doing the wrong thing.

The 2022 resignation trends confirm just how much stress is involved in workplace social interaction. Large numbers of people are quitting because they do not want to go back to the office. There are other factors such as commuting and schedule flexibility, but the allure of face-to-face teamwork doesn't seem to be an incentive to come back to the office. Data from Slack's (2022) ongoing survey of 10,000 knowledge workers found that with a third of them now back in the office five days a week, their work-related stress and anxiety has reached its highest level since the survey began in 2020.

This is a serious psychosocial hazard. It is not restricted to highly sensitive people. In a conversation with safety and health professional, Ron Gantt, he gets to the center of the matter.

> Why is social interaction a risk? This gets at the coordination dilemma we face. How do I know how you'll respond when I do something? Their response is critical to the success of whatever I'm doing. It could be something as simple as ordering coffee (how do I know that the barista will give me coffee for my money and actually give me what I want?) or as complex as telling your boss bad news. We can't read minds and we can't tell the future. But we sort of need both of those attributes to successfully function as individuals and as a society. The reason why going into detail on the nature of the risk Goffman is speaking about is critical is because it shows that we aren't just talking about people being 'soft.' This isn't just people who are more sensitive. This is everyone. Every interaction is risky. The only question is how risky and whether we are going to choose to support people in taking these risks.

Interacting with peers is just as risky as interacting with people in authority. Stephen Shorrock (2016), an interdisciplinary humanistic, systems and design practitioner who is interested in human work from many perspectives.

He worked in air traffic control safety for many years. We were in a conversation about just culture, psychological safety and learning. He said that often external investigators are accused of shutting down open communication because they are looking for someone to blame. But the real fear is about losing the approval of your colleagues—those closest to you. Air traffic controllers are more afraid of their colleagues than the investigator. They are the ones there every day. They know you and can expose your weaknesses. You can fool the investigator but you can't slide by the people you work with.

Develop emotional capacity for interpersonal risk

We are expected to speak up when we see something happening that is wrong. Those who are successful, even in the presence of authority, have an emotional capacity that others lack (Martha Acosta, 2021). If they do feel stressed they recover from it quickly. They might also be able to maintain their relationship with the person involved.

Acosta also states that the greater our emotional capacity for interpersonal risk, the greater our comfort with being authentic. From personal experience I am not sure that our comfort with being authentic translates into political power in the workplace. I have had encounters where being my authentic self has triggered anger and defensiveness in others. I had a particularly difficult experience with two white men from the nuclear industry who would cut me off and criticize me saying that they didn't like my tone of voice. My usual strategies for defusing conflict did not work.

We are very far from allowing a woman and even more so a woman of color to penetrate the defenses of those in authority. I found that setting personal boundaries around acceptable behavior in social interaction is very important and difficult for a woman of color. In my executive coaching I frequently work with such women. One of the development areas frequently mentioned is, "Can you help her communicate in a less emotional way. People think she is angry or attacking them." This is very frustrating for my Black and Latino clients because they come from a culture of emotional expression where people do not need to have difficult conversations after an emotional exchange. It is not surprising that Martha Acosta, a woman of color, is the one exploring this aspect of leadership communication.

Better than thick skin

Viola Davis, academy award winner and a Black woman, describes her epiphany.

> They tell you to develop a thick skin so things don't get to you. What they don't tell you is that your thick skin will keep everything from getting out, too. Love, intimacy, vulnerability.

I don't want that. Thick skin doesn't work anymore. I want to be transparent and translucent. For that to work, I won't own other people's shortcomings and criticisms. I won't put what you say about me on my load.

(Brown, 2018)

As long as we rely on others' reactions to judge ourselves or decide what we can say or not say we will have limited emotional capacity. Most of it will go to reinforcing our protective walls. The day we can truly stand outside ourselves watching and listening as unbiased observers we will be free from those limitations. That is what mindful and meditation practices are about. They build our capacity to remain in balance regardless of external reactions. From that stance we can easily see if we need to change our perspective or remain at peace with it.

Communication bridges

When you are speaking to another person you usually assume they are in your space and time. This is not a valid assumption. Most of us spend our time in the past or future while someone else is talking. Each of us has created a view or understanding of the world based on our experiences and our individual personalities. If you are speaking to many people at once, that is a daunting task. For you are speaking to a multiverse and the task of communicating is almost impossible. So let us better understand how communication takes place and what we can do that will improve our chances of success.

Until we invent the universal translator, communication takes time to set up because it doesn't exist outside of relationship. Relationship is the bridge to trust which is the bridge to communication.

Here we face yet another problem. When we meet someone new and have little experience with the tribe that they identify with, we do not know where the booby traps are. We do not know what will trigger fear and self-protective actions. It is easy to trigger a defense because humans have very sensitive antennas when it comes to threats to the Self. We treasure our identity and status. We've learned that without it, life is so much harder.

If you are a white male with a doctorate degree from Harvard University you might not know what I am talking about. Not unless you're Jewish. On the other hand if you are a dark-skinned woman with little education, very few bridges are available to you.

Bridges come built in for certain people. They don't realize it because they've always had them. If you've had to build your own you are very aware of it. That's not to say that everyone doesn't have to build bridges now and then. But that depends on whether you feel a need to connect with people that are different from you.

For instance, if you are wealthy and well educated you might feel a need to connect with people from different levels of society to better understand the world and yourself. Saint Francis of Assisi comes to my mind. He left his wealthy family to live a simple life of poverty to take care of others. There is a reason he's called a saint and that Mother Teresa is a saint. Leaving a comfortable life to enter a world of suffering and poverty isn't the easiest or the most likely thing to happen.

I've had to build bridges all my life but I can't say that's made me an expert. I still fall into the trap of thinking that a connection exists where there is none. What a shock it is when I reach out to someone and they treat me as not worthy. Perhaps one day I'll learn to not get angry. Perhaps one day I will truly know that what they say and do is not about me and has no impact on who I am.

I am better at it at 71, but I am no saint. A friend once told me to consider how all this bridge building has made me stronger and how it has contributed to my success. That's the standard rationalization to explain the purpose of suffering. Evolution created our capacity to suffer so that we might adapt and evolve. Apparently evolution doesn't believe in Appreciative Inquiry. I wonder if I would be even more powerful and have access to more of my gifts if I hadn't spent so much energy on building bridges?

It is hard to build a bridge. The hard part is the hesitation and fear that precedes getting started. Once I start sometimes it is easy and sometimes it is painful and hard. I tried to build a relationship with a partner for five years and swore I would not give up. In retrospect I should have walked away the first week. Sticking with it isn't always the best idea. The problem is knowing when it is and when it is not.

Oh, but I learned so much by sticking with it. How is that supposed to be a consolation? Even now I feel my greatest learning was that I truly lacked self-esteem. That is why deciding to build a bridge is so hard, I don't want to arrive at a place where you have to decide to let go and watch the bridge collapsing under your feet, falling into nothingness.

At least, I have finally developed some compassion for my antics. We're born knowing what the threat of losing a relationship looks and feels like. Lucky is the one who grows up in a situation where they are given the love and caring that makes it all endurable. For the really lucky it gives them a pathway to joy and wellbeing. Perhaps that is what happened with Saint Francis and Mother Teresa who grew up in wealthy families.

For those of us who are willing to take the risk of building a bridge with someone who is different from us, the social and psychological barriers can be daunting. There is no simple or quick solution. However, there are some bridge-building strategies to explore such as one-on-one conversations between boss and direct report, inter-disciplinary conversation skills, Confrontation Meetings, Fish Bowls and Rapid Relationality. They all involve conversation and piercing our social identity, which some may call our ego, via creating a setting where people feel heard and seen. Almost all communication work between people of different social fields involves finding ways to get around the ego and our fear of possible rejection.

Bridge building strategies

Conversation is the vehicle that drives and directs organizational life. What happens in organizations is not controlled by strategic planning, rewards, measurements or other management controls. Instead, it is the result of unpredictable interaction and communication between individuals and within groups. This is true because perceptions are influenced by conversations and power politics. Since the interactions and the exact nature of the problems that will emerge are unpredictable, an effective manager builds and maintains a wide range of relationships to maintain their knowledge and influence over what people are communicating to each other. The CEO needs to leverage their power to ensure communication connectivity. The example of Paul O'Neill when he was CEO at Alcoa in Chapter 6 serves to illustrate how power can influence the conversation, but only at the local level. If O'Neill had not made his direct reports accountable for communicating injuries, the attention of other managers would not have been on safety.

Described are three strategies known to be highly successful: (1) the *Confrontation Meeting* by Beckhard; (2) Inter*disciplinary Conversation* by Marinus and (3) *Rapid Relationality* by DiBenigno.

Richard Beckhard's confrontation meeting

Confrontation Meeting is not the best name for an event meant to improve trust and communication between conflicting groups. But that's the way things were in the 1960s when Richard Beckhard became instantly famous after publishing "The Confrontation Meeting" in the *Harvard Business Review* (1967).

Beckhard's point was that there are a lot of opinions, feelings and misinterpretations being talked about in the organization, but no one wants to talk about them openly. In the confrontation meetings that I facilitated, employees would freely write up all of their frustrations with supervisors and managers within their own peer groups and when they were asked to write the issues that they knew management would bring up, they were quite able to do it.

They thought these feelings were invisible if they were left unsaid. Imagine their surprise when each group found out the other group knew all about their frustrations. And without having to spy on them. Feelings and emotions, even thoughts are contagious in the human system. When they are made public, they lose half their power. The other half is lost when each group addresses and responds to those concerns in a respectful way. The risk you face in using this approach is first, not allowing the session to fall into blaming. The other risk is that it will raise expectations. If earnest efforts aren't perceived to deliver improvements, conditions actually worsen. For this reason the follow-up plan is critical.

Interdisciplinary conversations

James Marinus participated in a case study of a near-drowning incident during an Extra-Vehicular Activity (EVA 23) at the International Space Station (ISS). That means an astronaut was conducting an external repair in space when water began to accumulate inside of his space helmet. When it encroached his nose and mouth he began to drown. A well-executed rapid reentry to the ISS prevented the drowning. The after-incident review revealed several facts that provided an opportunity for learning.

The same thing had happened to an astronaut's helmet during the previous spacewalk. And even though the cause was not well understood, each team member suggested that a second spacewalk should go ahead as planned.

As always with hindsight, one asks how is that possible? Normally, they would have called for a delay of the spacewalk due to uncertainty. But they did not realize it until the review following the second incident. The mission support team discovered that collectively they had the technical and situational knowledge to predict that breath might condense into water and threaten the astronaut's life. In the debrief they found out that each of them had assumed the other had the information to make a safe decision.

More precisely, the crew members assumed the (EVA) manager was the integrator—sharing information among team members. The EVA manager assumed that mission support and crew members were synthesizing information with each other.

The sharing of information across different disciplines is not typical. Even though they are called an interdisciplinary team, they tend to work in multidisciplinary silos. Marinus suggested that in the future the teams would benefit if the EVA manager facilitated interdisciplinary conversations during risk-critical periods of uncertainty.

Curious, I asked Marinus how that would have improved the situation. He responded, "I would have made sure team members were talking to each other and watched for quality of interaction. Are they listening and processing? Are they learning from each other? Are they bringing in other disciplines? Are they excluding things?" Marinus agreed that most managers would not know how to notice or interpret such interactions.

Do senior leaders understand the importance of interdisciplinary conversations and the necessary skills to facilitate them? Marinus finds that some do but can't get the support to allocate the time needed to make this type of learning part of the work. In fact, some have experienced negative consequences from involving other disciplines in their projects. It led to more complex procedures that take time away from the real work—experimentation and research.

However, it doesn't have to be that way. Marinus demonstrated how an inter-disciplinary conversation can cut away clutter. The team took a 12-page procedure on how to start a class four laser and turned it into a one-page pictograph that everyone was happy with. Collaboration across disciplines can simplify work and make it safer. Getting disciplines to collaborate might require senior leadership intervention if the department heads are not on board.

Rapid relationality: how experts can build trust with line managers

This process addresses how to improve the levels of trust and communication between line managers and the support or helping functions. That could be HR, OD, IT, environmental, safety and health.

The Rapid Relationality process was developed in a landmark study where DiBenigno studied the introduction of mental health services in the U.S. Army. Over the last decade, soldiers' mental health problems have increased dramatically in the army. The worst areas have been posttraumatic stress disorder (PTSD) and suicide. Mental health problems were a "career ender" until they began to think of mental illness as invisible wounds that would be treated the same as physical injuries. In fact, soldiers could remain on active duty in their units while recovering (DiBenigno, 2021).

Unfortunately, the health providers often felt dismissed and excluded. DiBenigno was asked to come in and help. After many interviews she saw that the professional identities of commanders and health staff were at the root of the conflict. The commanders saw themselves as fielding a mission ready force and mental health providers saw themselves as providing rehabilitative care to soldiers. The commanders saw the mental health providers as Berkely Hippies.

The mental health providers were *peripheral experts*, someone hired for their expertise, but not seen as core to the organization's central mission. Their challenge is influencing core members to follow their expert recommendations. She saw the challenge and solution as helping the commanders and mental health providers to build relationships with each other.

The rapid relationality process provides opportunities for people with differing opinions or approaches to problem-solving to personalize their relationships. By spending time together they get to know each other to get beyond stereotypes. However, the time it takes to build relationships depends on the expert's personal characteristics—the main one being gender.

> My analysis (of the rapid relationality process) suggests it is not only what peripheral experts do that allows them to elicit cooperation from line managers but also when and how quickly they do it that matters. …. I further find that some experts have fewer tactics available to them or must use more time-consuming and energy-intensive tactics than others to achieve the same relational influence based on their personal characteristics (e.g.,

gender). As a result, it may be harder for some experts to achieve relational influence before their window of opportunity closes.

Julia DiBenigno (2021: 1)

Members of groups with different identities cannot influence change with each other until they build a relationship. Building these helping relationships takes time and requires asking questions to learn enough about the work and the systems to understand where people need or want help. In this case social gatherings provided that opportunity.

DiBenigno's process takes into account differentials in power. According to her observations the line manager resists the expert's recommendations because they do not see them as understanding the core business. Thus, their recommendations may interfere with the mission.

The peripheral expert who lacks authority and knowledge of interest to the manager may rapidly establish a relationship in three phases.

- Phase 1: rapidly getting in.
- Phase 2: rapidly proving oneself.
- Phase 3: continuously using relational expertise.

See Appendix C for full description of each phase.

Managing and influencing political relationships

Support functions have no direct authority. So any change initiated from there requires alliances with relevant leaders. But, a sole focus on leadership misses the mark. We could presuppose managers have authority, but they don't always have the kind of power that can get access to resources and the attention of other influencers. A power base comes from controlling an area of essential need such as money, information or other access to decision makers (French & Raven, 1959). When looking for alliances consider that the sources of power can come from:

- Control of scarce resources,
- Control of the decision-making process,
- Control of knowledge and information,
- The ability to stabilize discontinuous or unpredictable situations
- Control of technology
- Interpersonal alliances and networks
- Gender, family, ethnicity or race (These are a source of power if an organization is dominated by one or another.)

Correctly assessing the political backing for an improvement effort determines success or failure. Being able to identify and enroll the support of

Table 5 Sample. Political support chart

Name	Make it happen	Help it happen	Let it happen	None needed	Against
Joe P.	0 X				
Ariel L.	0				X
Sandra R.	0		X		
Santiago C.				0	X
Julie R.		0	X		

O = desired support and X = current support

those with power is part of change management. The political support chart can guide a conversation with your allies to plan your political strategy. It is adapted from Beckhard and Harris (1987). In the first column make a list of the people that need to support the project. Keep in mind that you may need different types of support from different players (Table 5).

How to create a political support chart:

Step 1: Make a six-column table.
Step 2: Enter the players in the "first column." Label the other column headings: "Make It Happen," "Help It Happen." "Let It Happen," "No Commitment" and "Against."
Step 3: For each player, determine the minimum level of commitment that is necessary for success. Mark an "O" in the respective column box.
Step 4: After locating the desired state "O" for a stakeholder, you then locate the present state and mark the box with an "X."
Step 5: Develop a strategy to move everyone to the desired state of commitment.

Explanation of the chart

In the above scenario Joe P is where we need him to be so the 0X are in the same spot. Ariel is against our plan and we need to move her into helping it happen. Julie is willing to let it happen but we need to enlist her support to make it happen. Santiago is against it, but we only need for him to let it happen. Our biggest challenge is Ariel because she is against it and we need her help to make it happen.

Gathering political support for an initiative

Next is planning how to influence the key players to support the initiative. If we look at the list of potential sources of powers above, each one can provide direction on how to approach each player. In Table 6, *Strategizing for political allies*, the first column indicates the source of power of a potential ally. The second column recommends how to influence them.

Table 6 Strategizing for political allies

In all cases begin by establishing a relationship with your potential ally	
Ally's source of power	Strategy examples
Control of scarce resources and funds	Put together the business case by relating the goals of the intervention to financial benefits. If a purpose or mission motivates this person, it would be important to know that and address how the initiative fits into what they already support
Control of the decision-making process	Prefers what style of decision-making? Analytical or Emotional? Present the argument to fit
Control of knowledge and information	Learn as much as you can about what they know. How was it acquired? How has it contributed to the success of the company? Show how the initiative will utilize their knowledge and include them in the process. Perhaps this initiative will help them increase their power
The ability to stabilize discontinuous or unpredictable situations	Learn how these abilities have been important and present why they are important to the success of the initiative
Control of technology	How will your approach enhance the value of the technology?
Interpersonal alliances and networks	How will their support strengthen and expand their network?
Gender, family, ethnicity or race	If you are not a member of this group, the first step would be to get the support of a person who is

Bibliography

Acosta, M. L. (2021). Vicious or virtuous: Exploring whether cognitive and emotional capabilities predict a manager's reaction to organizational paradox. Doctor of education dissertation George Washington University. https://www.proquest.com/openview/be2d5111c1182b325f59cc58b8e41e3e/1?pq-origsite=gscholar&cbl=18750&diss=y

Argyris, C., & Schon, D. (1974). *Theory in practice. Increasing professional effectiveness.* Jossey-Bass: San Francisco, CA.

Beckhard, R. (1967). The confrontation meeting. *Harvard Business Review.*

Beckhard, R., & Harris, R. T. (1987). *Organizational transitions: Managing complex change.* 2nd ed. Addison Wesley: New York.

Brown, B. (2018). Courage and power from pain. Accessed May 15, 2022. https://brenebrown.com/articles/2018/05/09/courage-power-pain-interview-viola-davis/

DiBenigno, J. (2021). Anchored personalization in managing goal conflict between professional groups: The case of U.S. Army Mental Health Care. *Administrative Science Quarterly, 63*(3), 526–569. Accessed April 28, 2022. https://drive.google.com/file/d/1hPwFtT18dMGq_x1bQktkRZPXf0nhlko_/view

French, J. R. P., & Raven, B. (1959). The bases of social power. In D. Cartwright (Ed.), *Studies in social power.* Institute for Social Research: Ann Arbor, MI (pp. 259–269).

Shorrock, S. (2016). Just culture: Who are we really afraid of? *Humanistic Systems Blog.* Accessed May 19, 2022. https://humanisticsystems.com/2016/11/24/just-culture-who-are-we-really-afraid-of%EF%BB%BF/

Slack. (2022). Future forum pulse. Return-to-office policies are hammering employee experience scores Accessed May 12, 2022. https://futureforum.com/

9 Health and safety—an emergent leadership strategy

- The H&S advisor's role in the future of work
- Raising the status and ROI of health and safety contributions
- Establishing the leadership of H&S at the executive level

A leadership opportunity for H&S managers and executives has risen from the convergence of a worldwide pandemic, a movement for social justice and growing demand for businesses to protect both workers and the public. It is the opening for H&S to be seen as a core business process. It is also about seizing the moment to recreate accident prevention as an equitable, adaptive and effective process. However, H&S advisors are concerned about assuming more responsibilities to take care of people. Some ask who is concerned about their PS and mental health? That is a fair question and that is one of the primary reasons for H&S occupying a leadership seat at the business table.

We explored various methodologies to successfully embed DEIB and PS into our organizations. It is a complex initiative that can only succeed through partnerships and coalitions. The events of Covid-19 opened an opportunity to recognize an existing partnership that is often overlooked and underutilized. I am talking about the contributions of H&S advisors that often go unnoticed. My conviction comes from years of intimate conversations one on one and in small groups with H&S advisors from many different countries. I've come to know their personal values, the ethic of caring, saving lives and the conviction to do the right thing. Some of them did not come into the profession with those intentions, but those who stayed were drawn into those values.

H&S advisors experience difficulty being heard and seen (Carrillo survey, 2022). Some are more successful than others, but they continue to work at establishing relationships and avenues of communication to protect employees and the companies they serve. This is why in addition to risk management, most have a personal understanding of the need for equity, inclusion and belonging. There is also evidence that many feel excluded, not heard and under-appreciated.

Even before the topics of inclusion, belonging and PS became prevalent, there were discussions at safety conferences about the importance of listening,

DOI: 10.4324/9781003368724-9

being responsive and engendering trust in the workplace. The people I interacted with immediately connected with the truth that those ideas were completely related to accident prevention. In other words, most H&S professionals already play a key role in creating PS. It is not an added responsibility that requires a degree in psychology. Here's an example of what that looks like:

> During Covid-19, people feel uncertainty in what they have to do to be protected, what will happen especially when one of their colleagues shows positive Covid-19 test. Based on my experience in this period, all safety professionals need to stay connected with the employees, listening to their concerns and giving them the right advice until overcoming this pandemic.
>
> Senior H&S advisor, USA

As a result H&S advisors have social capital in the workplace that they could spend on promoting the principles behind DEIB which is related directly to lowering accidents in the workplace as discussed in Chapter 7. Also related to DEIB is PS and, hopefully by now the connection between PS, trust and open communication is clear. We cannot say it too often that without trust and communication you have an unsafe organization.

I am not suggesting that H&S advisors need to lead the DEIB initiative or have responsibility for PS added to their job description. Many are already practicing those concepts while remaining aware of the political pressures that drive profit and compliance.

> I work in construction and O&G. Turnarounds and projects with small completion windows and tight schedules are the norm. Contract and temporary personnel make up a very fluid workforce. Working yourself out of work is the nature of the job. There's no "organizational loyalty" given or received. Time is money and anything that negatively affects already impacted schedules is dealt with remorselessly.
>
> So where does "psychological safety" fit in here? How does "care" replace compliance (and profit)? I'm certainly not asserting that a caring, psychologically safe environment wouldn't be better. I just don't see how profiting from a new book restating the obvious changes my reality. **Contrary to what authors and psychologists seem to believe, attempting to create a safe (both physically and psychologically) environment is what safety professionals have always done.**"

There would be some serious obstacles to unleashing this underutilized potential. One is that many H&S advisors are on the verge of resigning because of work demands and lack of recognition. The other obstacle is the identity of the profession. A third would be their lack of education in advocacy and relationship building. Unless they are seen as core business partners and acquire those skills, they cannot be effective in gaining cooperation from line managers.

Without the change in identity and status H&S activities are typically seen as getting in the way of the core goals managers are judged on. No amount of selling and relationship building on the part of advisors will change that. Only senior leaders can transition H&S advisors into core business partners.

The daily work life of an H&S advisor

It is best to let experience speak for itself. Sam Goodman remarked in his book, *Safety Sucks* (2020).

> I am completely done with seeing safety professionals die young of heart attacks, strokes, or suicide. I am tired of watching people lose their relationships because of this job, I am over watching people suffer at work because we refuse to do anything about it, and I'm sick of witnessing the depression that exists within our profession. We simply pretend that the problem does not exist, all the while professionals are suffering.

Even before Covid-19 a quiet struggle was already brewing amongst safety professionals. The pandemic expedited a wave of resignations by H&S professionals who felt overworked, under supported and unappreciated given all the extra responsibilities they had during the pandemic. An interview with one H&S professional who resigned described some of these conditions.

> For a long time I did not leave my job because of excellent team mates. We constantly had checks and balances with each other. We recognised when one of us was becoming stressed and supported each other in the right way. We also deliberately made an effort to protect one another from the environment we were in, to prevent stress in the first place. Eventually I decided to leave and find a less toxic environment to work in and I am very happy.

In the following paragraphs I will be drawing from my conversations and my 30 years of experience with H&S managers and staff to talk about how the people attracted to this profession are the perfect candidates to support the transformation to inclusion, belonging and equity. There are people already doing the work who feel alone and unsupported. Some wise manager will read this and gather the H&S team for a conversation and discover people like the one who wrote this comment:

> I am looking for a job where I can try to do my best in these 2 areas, where people are the center and we want to learn from our daily operation based on a trust relationship. I think I'm still young, so I keep struggling and pushing forward on my organization and I try to not give up when I'm feeling alone on the field.
>
> 36 year old H&S advisor

Burnout, stress and resignation

In the past year many safety advisors experienced a toxic corporate culture, burnout and lack of mental health support. On the other hand, the pandemic was motivating to some as H&S advisors saw their value go up and their ability to contribute recognized. In so doing their social standing or status went up, and for some people that balanced out separation from family and other extra burdens they were carrying.

> You are looked to for advice. Interpreting mandates were front and center. Technical expert for Covid-19. It is our job to work with the business, help workers manage their stress. Know the tools, exercise, EAP, meditation. Helping others during Covid-19. you also have your own family that you are taking care of. Haz recognition, construction. Pushing the safety message while doing Covid-19. what does this mandate mean? How are people feeling. Are the vehicles safe when you share them? The additional burden was educating, responding to questions, designing new processes.

The majority felt stressed, some quit their jobs and many more are contemplating it. In the US the timing of the George Lloyd killing by police also had a powerful impact. The following comment captures the constant pressure and disappointment as each new Covid-19 wave hit.

> At the beginning of the pandemic many of us felt confident we knew what to do. fatigue and burnout came in part II. The first part was stressful. we heard about Delta and we dealt with that. Omnicron I saw people's energy drop. Deflated. I thought I was prepared…There is a price tag for PPE and illness days. People felt strained. Will this ever end? to vax or not was stressful. 3 fatalities from non vaxers. You feel deflated. physically and mentally exhausted and regular work doesn't go away. We need to be more mindful of mental health. A lot of people talking about it. Managers' goals were to reduce absenteeism.
>
> Timing of George Lloyd killing and Covid-19 timing. For companies BLM too. It made it more challenging for companies. Even more reason to provide resources. SHE pro can't take things personally, not everyone can be an SHE prof.
>
> I think all safety professionals faced burnout but they differ in the degree they faced especially during Covid-19. During this period, people feel uncertainty in what they have to do to be protected, what will happen especially when one of their colleagues shows positive Covid-19 test. Based on my experience in this period, all safety professionals need to stay connected with the employees, listening to their concerns and giving them the right advice until overcoming this pandemic.
>
> Kenneth Wade, Senior EHS Director, USA

Indeed the situation felt like a proverbial last straw would bring everything tumbling down. There was really nothing to be done but act on the daily news and try to help people protect themselves as best as possible. For some it became unbearable so they resigned. Many more thought about quitting. Some people felt appreciated. Without any statistics to prove it, I suspect that was one of the reasons why not everyone quit.

I conducted a survey (May 2022) to learn more about the H&S advisor's experience during Covid-19 (See Table 6) and received 59 responses. Judging by the number of likes on the following comment, it likely represents the experience of many who quit or thought about quitting.

> I experienced burn out in 2021 and actually left my job due to it and its effect on my family life. There was a combination of many factors. The increased work load due to Covid-19, unrealistic leadership expectations, and more, led to me feeling tired and unvalued – which led to a poor family life too. My learnings: You can help create psychological safety at your work by being vulnerable yourself BUT you can also show commitment to your own wellbeing by walking away if needed (I appreciate not everyone has the good fortune to just quit a job). I believe the last few years have revealed the true nature of leaders and the workplace….and some of it is ugly.

The pressure and stress in this job are both legal and emotional as described by an H&S manager:

> In health and safety burnout pressures are both legal and emotional. Every safety manager knows that after a serious accident there will be an investigation and they could be found liable. So you have both the emotional baggage because someone got hurt under your care and you have the stress of the potential legal liability. This constant stress eventually causes burnout.

Earlier I cited a study that found a Toxic Culture was the #1 reason for resignation. My survey matched those results as shown in Figure 9 indicating that the #1 reason for stress and burnout during Covid-19 was a toxic culture. Other causes were disrespect, lack of autonomy, insufficient resources and fear of the negative impact on mental health.

Also matching the global statistics, about 50% of those who participated said they thought about quitting, but very few considered leaving the profession.

Figure 9 lists the 16 stressors that H&S Advisor named as reasons for burnout during Covid-19. The two categories that stand out are concerns about personal mental health and the effects of a toxic culture.

Table 6 Questionnaire for H&S Covid-19 stressors

H&S advisor survey questions N = 60	*% yes responses*
1 Did you suffer work-related burnout or stress in the last year?	96%
2 Did you consider quitting your job in the last year?	50%
3 Have you quit your job and found another in the same role?	12%
	3% about to
4 Have you left the profession?	2%

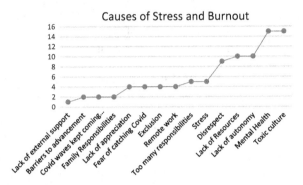

Figure 9 What were the main causes of burnout and stress for safety advisors during Covid-19.

Strong ethic of responsibility

> In safety for 20 years and always been motivated to help people. I nearly quit…more than once. But I still feel safety people can improve they just lack the light to show the way.
>
> Safety Advisor

Those who left their job in 2021 due to burnout remarked that it not only affected them but also their family life. There was a combination of many factors but the increased workload and unrealistic expectations from management left some feeling tired and undervalued. This eventually leaked over into the family life affecting everyone.

Safety advisors faced additional risks themselves and felt the responsibility for protecting employees. During Covid management was gone but they were there, as essential employees and they represented and ethic of caring to those who were also risking themselves.

> I don't feel that many realize the importance of the safety professional's role in the workplace. Being present and available is a comfort to workers because they know that you are doing everything in your power to help them.

Now, even though the virus is not eradicated, it has slowed down enough to contemplate a different way to move forward. Some feel that the pandemic was an opportunity for managers to fully appreciate the value of H&S advisors. And because of the nature of the people attracted to the profession there is plenty there to start anew—to recognize the full potential of the H&S advisor to help managers meet the socio emotional needs of employees. As we discussed, not meeting the social needs would mean the loss of valuable talent. But, first we have some work to do to reposition the social identity of H&S advisors as core contributors to organizational performance.

Shift to core business identity and status

Feeling excluded and undervalued is a major cause of stress for H&S professionals. They are not alone. Like mental health workers or environmental experts
they are hired for an expertise that others do not see as core to the organization's
central purpose. They are *peripheral experts* whose challenge is influencing core
business leaders to follow their expert recommendations (DiBenigno, 2017).

There were failed attempts to change the status of expert advisors by providing new titles or having them report directly to the CEO. It did not
increase their influence on the operational leaders. DiBenigno 's research
provided a key insight that explains why it did not work. She came to the
conclusion that the reason these experts were excluded from core group status
was their professional identity.

When you look at it in that way it makes sense that one's position on the
organizational chart doesn't change status because proximity doesn't affect
your relationship with the people who hold power. Social identity determines your status and membership. More recently corporations have placed a
respected operational leader as the head of H&S. Such a candidate brings with
them their prior relationships to power so that the first hurdle to be seen as
a member of the core mission is successfully met. The second hurdle would
be developing relationships with the H&S community that would allow for
mutual influence on the way they think about safety improvement.

Both professional and social identity speeds up or slows down the ability
of the expert to build a relationship. In DiBenigno's study she was able to
observe that the more the mental health expert and the commander had in
common and the more the commander valued the expert's background, the
faster they were able to connect. This is why gender, race, socio-economic
status and cultural background represent obstacles to being seen and heard by
people in positions of higher authority.

Another way that a peripheral expert attempts to influence is by presenting
data to show effects on the bottom line. In a few studies it was found that the
financial data makes no difference unless there is an established relationship
first (Howard-Grenville, 2003). For example, an operations manager who
becomes safety director could succeed because they bring all their prior relationships with them.

Examining the current identity of H&S advisors

Regardless of how H&S advisors see their role in the organization, there is a
recurring theme of opposition between them and line managers. John Green,
an H&S executive for several corporations, observed that the opposition is a false
dichotomy. H&S advisors see a condition as a problem needing to be eliminated,
rather than seeing it as an actuality and trying to live with it or accommodate it.

We often see safety and operational goals as conflicting but instead of
accepting this and working out how best to support successful outcomes

when these goals conflict (safety might be more important when we have lots of time but less so when we are up against time pressures) we simply claim that shouldn't be so and that something dreadful will happen unless we resolve the conflict....

John Green, Senior Vice President Global HSSE at SNC-Lavalin

Are there ambiguous situations that cannot be eliminated if work is to be completed? Is it possible to believe that zero incidents are an impossible goal while also believing that the company is obligated to do its best to prevent harm to employees, the community and the environment?

What is the fear behind saying that safety can't always be number one? Is it fear of being co-opted by assuming an operational goal such as meeting production deadlines? Is it fear that it means trying to fit in to be accepted? While forming relationships can lead to line managers adopting recommendations, there is a danger of reinforcing the very system that disadvantages H&S advisors. Thus, potentially limiting more radical change in the organization's culture and power structure as expressed in the following comment:

There is a learned helplessness that comes with working in the area of safety. Those in charge of safety do so more to control against "too much safety" or "doing anything that might impact operations." They listen without hearing and judge without understanding. They spew buzzwords like a marketing plan on steroids, creating an illusion of competence that doesn't exist. When challenged, they agree and do nothing, hoping the question will disappear in a fog of wordsoup. They ... undermine trust. They remain in those positions because they're good for the bottom line...the bloody one we used to talk about.

Former S & H advisor

So, how do H&S advisors see themselves? There isn't one profile for an H&S advisor. I conducted a small online survey asking how safety advisors would describe their role. There was high consensus around being an advisor, leader and researcher/student/learner. There was still significant but less consensus around teacher and technical expert as shown in Table 7.

Table 7 Respondents were asked to agree or disagree with a list of role descriptions

H&S role descriptor	% agree or strongly agree
1 Advisor	95
2 I am a leader	95
3 I am a researcher, student or learner	92
4 I am a teacher	78
5 I am a technical expert	73
6 I am a protector	52
7 I am a healer	50

$N = 60$; 55% masculine; 38% feminine; 8% binary

The roles of protector and healer only received 50% agreement. I was surprised as I certainly thought these archetypes would resonate with them. The explanation I received is that they were too patriarchal. I don't agree from a Jungian perspective, however I understand given the pressure to be professional and rational.

Transitioning H&S professional identity and curriculum

If the stress level of your job has left you worried about your mental health, what are the alternatives? One solution is to quit H&S and go into another profession. Another is to reshape the job you are in or find a company that will give you the role you want. Yet another is to reconsider how you frame your purpose. Taking the top four roles that H&S advisors chose: advisor, leader, learner and teacher (Table 7) one possibility is adopting the broader identity of helping profession. The main benefit I see is that it would reframe the curriculum to better prepare the H&S advisor to work with people.

This would apply to the H&S advisor that works directly with employees, those that educate them and those behind the scenes that do research and design. It can be argued that the *helping* aspect is an integral part of H&S work. The first rule of helping is *Do no harm*. That certainly applies here.

One of the aspects of the work that helping professionals perform is that it explicitly aims to change another. Again this applies to those working in H&S because advisors are expected to raise awareness and improve safety-related behaviors. The helping occupations also have values and principles that attract others into the profession. Trust, respect and congruence are major components of a good helping relationship. The safety advisors I have met would have no trouble agreeing that these were aspects of the profession that attracted them to join.

Of the five stages of the helping process four of them bear a striking similarity to the work of H&S advisors: (1) establishing a working relationship; (2) assessing or defining the present problem; (3) identifying and setting goals; (4) choosing and initiating solutions. The fifth step is planning and introducing termination and follow-up, which could be replaced in H&S with *follow up and measure progress*. Currently H&S advisors use Plan, Do, Check, Act (PDCA), which does not really capture the relational aspect of their work. Thinking of it as part of the helping professions could reshape a relevant curriculum and align more closely with the reality of the work.

Establishing the H&S leadership role

As H&S advisors are asked to do more and more to take care of people, some ask, "Who is concerned about our psychological safety and mental health?" That is a fair question. It is a management's responsibility to be concerned about employee H&S. However, the best answer is "you are" because that is where you have the most control. This matter of PS manifests as feeling secure, respected and a part of the team. We were born with inherent ability to connect with others. We need only peel away the layers of fear that keep us from expressing it. In the case of approaching those in higher positions of power you need to approach without defensiveness. Defensiveness provokes negative outcomes. Humble inquiry always opens new doors to trust and open communication.

With that said, the current status of H&S advisors does not make it possible for them to make themselves part of the core business and sell their ideas to improve wellness in the workplace. This will need to be done at the highest level of the organization. The *rapid relationality process* described in Chapter 8 can improve the acceptance levels of the advisor by line management. However, any transformational change in H&S identity and status would require leadership from the senior executive ranks. It would seem a logical step for a forward-thinking senior leadership team to take this step to unleash the talent of this profession that attracts such remarkable people.

It is normal in the cycle of life for what has been empty to become full and for what has been full to become empty. The pandemic took its toll and drained our wellbeing, as well as our economic and healthcare support services. We can choose how to refill that void. Repositioning the H&S advisor as a core business partner would benefit organizations in several ways. An important one would be improved working conditions for people who take on the role. A second would be removing obstacles to implementing H&S expertise. A third is leveraging the social capital of the H&S advisor to promote inclusion.

Bibliography

Carrillo, R. A. (2022). H&S Advisor covid experience survey.

DiBenigno, J. (2017). Anchored Personalization in Managing Goal Conflict between Professional Groups: The Case of U.S. Army Mental Health Care. Administrative Science Quarterly. Vol. 63(3)526–569. Accessed 4/28/2022. https://drive.google.com/file/d/1hPwFtT18dMGq_x1bQktkRZPXf0nhlko_/view

Goodman, S. (2020). *Safety Sucks*. Hominum: MA.

Howard-Grenville, J. A., & Hoffman, A. J. (2003). The importance of cultural framing to the success of social initiatives in business. *Academy of Management Executive, 17,* 70–84.

10 Getting to inclusion and belonging

- Bringing along an organization to Inclusion and Belonging is a personal journey of self-actualization
- Finding your identity and where you belong
- Knowing and accepting that it all begins with you
- Enactment

> My greatest insight after years of conducting organizational learning projects and facilitating corporate change is that the success of an intervention depends on the interior condition of the intervener.
>
> (Scharmer, 2007: 7) Bill O'Brien, CEO of Hanover Insurance

Bill O'Brien wasn't the first person to make the observation that change begins with us. But he is a credible witness and practitioner. There's a lot we have to muddle through in the beginning of a transformation. There are political pressures to please those with power. There is also self-interest to think about. How many of us can afford to say "Take this Job and shove it!" Perhaps that is only the province of rich musicians and songwriters (Figure 10).

Those who have been successful in creating change report similar paths. The struggle of not being seen and heard, the difficulty of accepting that we have no control over anything except our thoughts and emotions. And then having the humility to accept that we must take incremental steps and enjoy our small successes. Getting to the top takes a steady vision and strong values.

Hanover was also practical. He placed skepticism in the middle of the journey. But, in reality we face it from the very beginning because many of us have difficulty believing that all people are willing and able to contribute to the success of the organization. There were times when I felt surrounded by resistors. I am guilty of doubting that things could ever change.

One day I found myself surrounded by willing practitioners, employees, friends and colleagues. Step-by-step I had to realize that people around me were not changing, it was me. The same union members were in my sessions. The same managers and supervisors with different priorities were there as

DOI: 10.4324/9781003368724-10

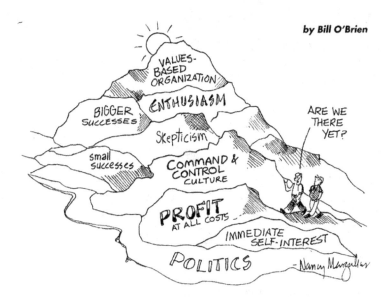

Figure 10 It's a journey (Automattic.com).

well. My mom used to say we are always confronting the same relationship issues; they are just wearing different clothes. If you want to have a different experience the solution is to change yourself.

It starts with me

Each chapter in this book represents a guide for leading an organization toward inclusion and belonging. Getting there is a moral responsibility. If we are to succeed in changing our corporate communities, each organization needs a network of managers who have paid attention to their own development, a subject seldom found in the curriculum of our business schools.

You have been presented with the case that it is a leadership responsibility to create generative social fields (workspaces) where it is safe to be seen and heard. To do that you must go out, be vulnerable and interact with people. Organizational behavior follows the direction of powerful and salient role models.

Do not expect immediate results. This business about being seen and heard is risky. Invisibility feels safer sometimes. You might want to be recognized but you would rather wait until you are certain you are right or that you won't make mistakes. That is how I used to feel because I couldn't breathe or move when faced with the possibility of ridicule or criticism.

I had to learn that I have the right to be wrong, to fail and to learn from it all. I do not have to be perfect the first time around. But I am still not immune. While writing this book I felt I had to be very careful. When you say something that could make people re-think their beliefs even if you present many expert references, you can be ridiculed.

If you are a line manager and you find yourself unwilling or unable to assert a position that others do not support, then perhaps fear of not fitting in with those above you holds you back. I empathize. But when you find yourself hiding that which is essential to your nature, you are diminishing your potential to live a fulfilling life. Why does fitting in seem to be more important than living a fulfilling life? Neuroscience found an answer. Our brain is hard-wired to equate death with ejection from the tribe.

There is no need to feel ashamed of the need to belong. Recognize it and let it go. It is not always the best course to push for fellowship with a group that is making it too difficult to belong. It is correct to withdraw when those in positions of power oppose you or ignore you. But don't confuse it with running away. Running away means saving yourself at any cost. Withdrawal isn't giving up. It is a sign of strength, self-esteem and strategic thinking.

When you are feeling stressed or disrespected it is right to step back to a place of personal security so that you don't exhaust your inner resources. That way you will retain your energy for when it is time to make another effort to connect or influence.

Suffering and anxiety are optional

Many philosophers have delved into the question of free will and choice. Are the chemicals released in the body during extreme duress necessary for transformation? Bennis and Thomas found that to be true for the CEOs that they interviewed for the article, The crucibles of Leadership (2002). They proposed that one of the most reliable predictors of great leaders is the ability to learn from even the most negative experiences. They called these experiences crucibles that seemed to make leaders stronger and more confident. Appreciative Inquiry says the world has learned all it has to learn from suffering. Bad things happened to all of us, suffering is optional. You get to pick the path.

Many battles have been fought for external freedom, but what about internal freedom? Our emotions and memories of the past will take away our freedom if we let them. Our internal landscape can be a tough place to live when it is filled up with self-judgment and harsh criticism.

If you were not lucky enough to be born into a household that fostered belonging and mutual respect, the road might be long. But there is a road and you are not alone. A society that embraces DEIB begins with self-acceptance, the one place where we have the most control. We can learn from others who are also on this journey.

I've been acting as Covid-19 Officer alongside my normal job for the past 2 years. The only thing that helps is selfcare and a growth mindset.

Yes, I've experienced a lot of stress, but what kept me going was a constant lookout for the silver lining: more time with my family, learning from situations, room for strategic thinking, … And above all, the knowledge that I'm only in control my own feelings, thoughts and decisions.

There is only one way to happiness and that is to cease worrying about things which are beyond the power of our will.

(Epictetus) Kareem Ateff, AIFireE,
RSP Site HSE Mgr, Egypt

Applications of identity, belonging and inclusion to leadership

Everyone is looking for a place where they feel the sense of belonging and inclusion. It cannot be lost, it is always within you.

Identities are always connected to status and therefore voice. Doctors have a higher status than nurses. That makes it hard for nurses to point out mistakes to a doctor. They worry that if questioned, the doctor's word would be the one accepted. Higher status is usually connected to more power. A leader's status can influence how others see reality. That makes inclusion a powerful tool for them to create generative social fields, and exclusion a potent sanction. Self-awareness is key to using status wisely. The visibility and weight of words and actions increase with status, often in unintended ways.

Identities can unite or divide because they provide opportunities to include or exclude. Exclusion is hurtful if you want to belong but don't meet the requirements. It is also detrimental when the people excluded have the knowledge and experience that the group needs. In spite of the potential drawbacks the various types of identities are an essential component of psychological safety.

As a leader it is best to become acquainted with the identities of the people working with you. It is also a good idea to assess your professional identity because each one also carries a set of assumptions that may become a source of bias.

Introducing the concept of inclusion and belonging to groups with different identities requires self-awareness and the ability to empathize. In this effort you will be the main bridge for common understanding until others begin to emulate you.

Social identity is a label others put on you usually based on the way you look and your economic or social status. When I was growing up the USA used the term *Mexican-American*. I wanted to be just Mexican or American. I wanted to belong and be accepted, but both cultures rejected me. Being a Mexican-American was torture. Whoever thought of that name was trying to say, be proud of your ethnic identity regardless of how you are treated.

After doing a little research I found that I was right. The term emerged in the 1930s to promote assimilation of resistant Mexicans who were upset, for some reason, over the acquisition of their lands after the Mexican–American war. Then there were the "no Mexicans allowed" signs outside of restaurants in states that were previously owned by Mexico. Needless to say the addition of a hyphenated *American* doesn't reduce racism. But it does help the people in power categorize others into neat social identities.

Personal identities are also powerful but they come and go. I used to be a student, a kindergarten teacher and a musician in an orchestra. I'm not anymore. Other personal identities can attract ostracism. My birth father was never a part of my life and as a child I was made acutely aware that meant I was inferior. So, I made up stories that my father had died so that I could feel that I belonged. I learned I had to do this in a Mexican childhood game where we formed a circle holding hands. One unlucky girl would be chosen to play the orphan. She stood in the center of the circle and we sang, "La echaremos a la calle a sufrir su desventura...." We will throw her on the street so she can mourn her misfortune. There comes the trash collector now.

Nothing could communicate more strongly what it took to belong more than that song. I remember it as if it were yesterday. You cannot survive alone. You must belong to a family to receive any compassion or help. Even if you need it most when you are alone.

Each significant loss or personal disappointment involves the threat or loss of identity. It is not something that I look forward to or enjoy. I sometimes think I would feel more secure enmeshed in traditions and family responsibilities. But I know that is not my truth. If it were that is exactly where I would be now. The price of freedom and autonomy is ambiguity. I gladly pay the price, since living without them would be unbearable.

Professional identities: Personal identities change through life. Professional identities also can change. They are based on the knowledge, training and education you received. It can also depend on your experience using that knowledge and skills. Additionally there are associated values, ethics and workstyle behaviors—sometimes even ways of dressing.

The conflict between professional identities can be a serious obstacle to sharing of information. In some work settings if you do not have a Ph.D. people hold you in lower regard. In cultures that are technology focused, being a customer service representative would lower your status.

Voice: having it, losing it and finding it

Most of us are born with the ability to speak the truth without fear. There used to be a funny television show called *Candid Camera*. Young children would blurt out observations that would embarrass all adults. In one scene a shoe sales person was wearing a toupee and it kept sliding off. Finally the child asked, "Why is that man's hair falling off?" His mother quickly shushed him, and that is where the social training begins. It isn't always for the best to speak thoughts out loud. However, self-censoring is cause of much anxiety.

Lost and found

When we are excluded we lose our voice because no one is listening. I don't think you can skip the painful aspects of recovering your voice. I could not. Much of my energy went into protecting myself from humiliation or further ostracism. The truth is you never really lose your voice. It simply gets buried under the voices telling you've been ostracized and you need to figure out how to belong.

To get it back I had to identify the voices in my head. Which one was me? There were several that constantly reminded me that I could not trust anyone, so it was better not to say anything. But there was still a force within me seeking to be heard. The image that comes to mind is the blades of grass growing from the cracks in my concrete driveway. They are not flowers. They are weeds that we remove lest they damage the driveway further. But they come back because that is their nature. It is the same with voice. Sometimes it is the same person speaking up again, and sometimes it is a different one. But both represent nature's resilient power.

We cannot take that remarkable resilience for granted. There is a limit as to how many times even a weed can come back. We can see that in the wastelands that humans have created with nineteenth-century mines, wood-processing plants, landfills, large petrochemical complexes and nuclear weapons plants. We can also create wastelands in our organization because we're not listening.

In individualistic societies each of us is expected to recover our own voice. But sometimes we cannot do it alone. I feel gratitude to those people who dedicate their lives to noticing and helping people find their voice. We need to support people like that in our organizations if we don't want to end up losing people with talent simply waiting to be recognized.

The statistics on the percent of people in the helping professions that are planning to resign due to the stress are shocking. The causes are stress, burn-out and the lack of appreciation they feel. These are the people that nurture resilience in our society. In business we saw that senior women leaders provide this nurturing as do safety and health advisors and other support functions. It is a leadership responsibility to retain and support these employees.

Finding the middle road for voice

We are learning that the best performance comes from people working together in an environment where people can be authentic. It is because it is the only way people can contribute their full human potential. The dilemma is that saying whatever you want whenever you want to can destroy relationships. This is why self-awareness and having a framework for authenticity are so critical.

The first thing is to trust you already belong just the way you are. You may simply be in the wrong place. If you do not accept this, you will spend a lot of your energy trying to change things that you cannot change. I tried to change myself through many avenues like therapy, affirmations and exercises like Byron Katie's four questions for many years. That did not work. What did start to make a difference was a meditation.

> There is no place to go. There is nothing to do. There is nothing to change. There is nothing to fix, no expectations to meet. There is only now and you are complete. Each time a thought comes into your mind acknowledge it and let it go. If you let it go it will disappear.

After a while there is only silence in your mind. And you are instructed only to observe. I discovered that there are two I's. One is the I who cannot speak up for fear of exclusion. The other I observes and feels none of the restraints. Neither does it feel obligated to speak up. I would describe what happened as a freeing up of cognitive space in my brain.

I could reach a place in my mind that was free of all self-judgment and expectations. Free of the thoughts that reminded me of my failures, thoughts that would remind me that I did not belong and had been abandoned. The first time I was able to achieve a state of silence I felt an incredible sense of peace. I realized it was my own thoughts oppressing me. In the silence, I was free to let go of the thoughts that caused stress. After meditation I was able to keep thoughts that contributed to my wellbeing and the wellbeing of others, while letting go of those that did not.

It is possible to get good at letting go of thoughts that drain our energy. The more we can practice choosing our emotions the better we feel. The more we exercise, the more we want to exercise. The less we eat, the easier it is to eat less. The more we insist on being right and controlling others, the greater our disappointment and pain. The more we invest in gaining access to our inner peace, the more clarity we receive.

Having achieved a sense of peace and inner belonging we are ready to contemplate the wisdom of speaking or not speaking up. Before being in this state there are too many conflicting emotions that may push us to make wrong decisions. Three that come to mind are self-doubt, thinking that we can change someone else and third that our perception is the "truth."

Changing the world through the power of inclusion

> Everyone is seeking to escape from a prison others have made for them, but others do not keep them there. They can free themselves.

You may long to belong and then become frustrated with the limitations and requirements. There is no free lunch. Inclusion and belonging may produce freedom or bondage according to the way you use them. We may feel it is a human right to be accepted just as we are. That making judgments about who's in and who's out is inhumane. However, to be human includes judging, excluding, making assumptions and having biases.

One of my role models, Shirley Chisholm, started this journey and reached the top of the mountain to inclusion and belonging. She was the first African American woman elected to the House of Representatives. She was also the first black and first woman to run for President of the United States. When she announced her candidacy for president at the 1972 U.S. Democratic convention the delegates from Alabama, stood up and cheered for her. The political world was stunned because at the time George Wallace, a well-known racist, was governor of Alabama and also running for president.

In an interview Chisholm (2010) said she is still puzzled by their support and still does not believe that there was any intent to hurt her campaign. She also talks about her visit to George Wallace[1] in the hospital after he was shot. She almost lost her seat in the house of representatives because people were so angry that she would extend this humanitarian gesture to someone they considered an enemy.

When she walked in, according to her, Wallace sputtered, "What are you doing here? You shouldn't be here!" She said, "I am here because you are ill. And you are ill for a good reason. God guides us." The doctor asked her to leave, but Wallace held on to her hand tightly. He didn't want her to go.

On her way out she told one of her aides that she wanted to visit Wallace in the hospital because "...sometimes we have to remember we're all human beings...I may be able to teach him something to help him regain his humanity...One act of kindness may make all the difference in the world."

According to Capehart (2019), Wallace's daughter, Peggy Wallace Kennedy, said Chisholm's visit to the hospital "planted a seed of new beginnings in my father's heart." Over time, that seed bore fruit when Wallace publicly renounced segregation and sought the black community's forgiveness. He also appointed a record number of African Americans to fill state positions in his final term as governor.

Chisholm would say that when reaching a goal seems impossible and the situation looks dark, stay true to your Self. The situation may call for the saintly response of turning the other cheek. Returning blow for blow would only escalate the situation. This would take the ultimate degree of self-trust in taking right action.

In dealing with human matters, especially when trying to change long-standing attitudes and behaviors, one has to be able to accept reality for what it is, yet still act in accordance with one's vision. Chisholm acted according to her heart and beliefs even though she knew that many would scorn her when she visited Wallace. She had the choice of staying within the boundaries of what people expected from her but she chose to leave her safe cage and chase after her dream of ending segregation. Chisholm did not win the presidency, but her actions influenced Wallace to become one of the strongest voices upholding segregation to reverse his position. Sometimes we win even though we appear to have lost.

An inclusive leader like Shirley Chisholm does not appear to rely on a social identity to feel a sense of belonging or purpose. They are inclusive because they are able to let go of their own identity to identify with many different life experiences. They also seem to know and pay attention to the core needs of being human. I don't know why Wallace trusted Chisholm, but I know that she had a hand in transforming his fear of African-Americans into trust. She did it by giving him a gift that is very hard to come by, she believed him to be willing and capable of making his country a better place for everyone. I am sure many told her she was crazy. But I come back to the story in my prologue about Mr. Hall, the teacher who helped students in the ghetto excel in all their academics. Others tried to copy his techniques, but we all know that it wasn't the resources or the curriculum that made it happen. It was as his student said, "Mr. Hall believed we were smart. And then we were."

Enactment is the final step that leads to personal transformation

One can learn and have many insights but without enactment nothing changes. Most of us have heard this many times. So if we have yet to experience the success we desire, let's take some time to reflect on what it means to enact change by taking action. I use the word *enactment* with a serious purpose. We are talking about nothing less than personal transformation and it will not do to only talk about action plans and goals or targets.

Enactment per Karl Weick is people taking action to make sense of how things work and to solve problems (1988, 2009). It is also a way of approaching uncertainty. So enactment is a part of the learning process. Taking action sometimes leads to mistakes. Thus mistakes are also part of the learning process.

Enactment—taking action to solve a problem—creates a chain of events. Sometimes things go in the direction that you desire, sometimes they don't. These outcomes are only seen or understood after action has been taken. Sometimes even though you end up with a desirable outcome, in hindsight, by taking a different path you could have avoided some of the negative experiences.

Enactment takes patience. Why does it take so long to imbed the values of inclusion? Because in order to bring about such a transformation, management has to change some of its long-held beliefs and habits. People quickly grasp the intellectual dimension of these ideas, and the benefits. But earlier we talked about the anxiety and uncertainty raised by these challenges to long-held beliefs. Translating the ideas into practice takes quite a bit longer. There needs to be a safe place to wrestle with the personal implications of the new ideas.

Enactment brings ideas or visions into physical reality. I like this explanation of how to create change, because it means taking action is what changes the reality around us. That every action we take changes the situation we are facing. It is action that changes the course of intended outcomes. We need to pay attention to the conversations we are having because that is the most frequent opportunity to enact change.

Finally, organizational transformation really does start with us. Our behavior—the way we perform a task and the way we show up—is a form of enactment. Who we are naturally enacts our vision. Thus, inclusivity attracts talent. Exclusion pushes it away.

Note

1 George Wallace was governor of the state of Alabama in the US. 1970–1987.

Bibliography

Bennis, W., & Thomas, R. (2002). Crucibles of leadership. *Harvard Business Review, 80,* 39–45, 124.

Capehart, J. (2019). How segregationist George Wallace became a model for racial reconciliation: Voices of the movement, episode six. *Washington Post.* Accessed July 14, 2022. https://www.washingtonpost.com/opinions/2019/05/16/changed-minds-reconciliation-voices-movement-episode/

Chisholm, S. (2010). 1972 Bid for presidency. https://www.youtube.com/watch?v=qB_krfRLSVM

Scharmer, O. C. (2007). Introduction. Theory U: Leading from the future as it emerges. Accessed May 3, 2020. https://www.bkconnection.com/static/Theory_U_EXCERPT.pdf

Weick, K. (1988). Enacted sensemaking in crisis situations. *Journal of Management Studies, 24*(4). Accessed September 2, 2018. https://onlinelibrary.wiley.com/doi/pdf/10.1111/j.1467-6486.1988.tb00039

Weick, K. (2009). *Sensemaking in the organization.* Blackwell: Malden, MA.

Appendix A

Authentically inclusive leadership practices

Generative practice	Recipient's potential interpretation	Psychological safety need addressed
Ask questions rather than give direction or advice	*My competence is respected*	*Autonomy*
Extend trust, for example, giving people more autonomy in their roles	I am trusted to do my job	Autonomy
Insist on having dissenting points of view	I can speak up even if my boss or others might disagree	Autonomy/certainty
Use people's name	Recognition	Belonging
Look at people when you pass them and say hello	Recognition	Belonging
Listen and focus on understanding and learning	My manager /co-workers are willing to listen to me, I am valued	Belonging
Communicate your desire to connect personally with team members	My boss cares about me. They seem genuinely interested in getting to know me	Belonging
Meaningful immediate recognition—particularly with reference to the respective social identities	My boss/team recognize who I am for the team	Belonging/status
Empathetic listening	My boss/team members respect me and value my input. I feel seen and heard	Belonging/status
Encourage supportive practices among the team members	Trust building	Belonging/status/certainty
Lend your power and protection to raise the status of another	My manager/co-workers have my back. It is safe for me to take risks	Certainty
Share your story and emotions at the right moments	My boss is authentic and transparent, I can trust	Certainty
Frequent conversations to clarify priorities and direction	I am in the know. I can take initiative more confidently	Certainty
Provide timely information and decisions	I have what I need to succeed	Certainty

(Continued)

Generative practice	Recipient's potential interpretation	Psychological safety need addressed
Ask questions rather than give direction or advice	*My competence is respected*	*Autonomy*
Identify your values, speak about them, embody them	I trust my boss because they stand by their words and principles	Equity
Sincerely apologize when appropriate	My boss will admit it when he/she makes mistakes, I should do the same	Equity
Give credit for contributions	I am safe to contribute my best work	Equity
Stop texting or typing during conversations	I'm respected	Status
Build on each other's conversations. Resist the urge to disagree. Remember it isn't either/or. It is "And"	I feel heard	Status
Give thanks and recognition for specific contributions	I am important and my abilities are recognized	Status
Avoid criticism in public	Saving face	Status
Ask for feedback, offer to help and follow up	My manager /co-workers respect my views and can be trusted	Status
Regular conversations for career development and performance feedback	I am valued, I know where I stand	Status/certainty
Act on information, concerns and ideas received	Speaking up is safe and has value	Status/certainty

Appendix B

The confrontation meeting

Richard Beckhard 1967

Purpose

The confrontation meeting format allows participants to speak openly about topics usually unspoken. It provides top management with accurate information regarding an organization's health and the opportunity to make improvements with all managers present. Their engagement makes follow–up more likely.

1 **Climate setting: one hour**

In the very beginning, the top executive communicates to the entire management group his objectives for the meeting and his concern for and interest in open discussion and the problem facing the group.

2 **Information collection: one hour**

The entire group of employees is divided into small heterogeneous units consisting of seven to eight participants. If there is top management group it meets as a separate unit. No boss and subordinates are placed together. Each unit consists of participants from each functional area.

The assignments to these groups:

- Write one list of how you feel the other group(s) contribute to miscommunication and lack of trust.
- Write a second list of what you believe the other group(s) are writing about you.
- Each unit is advised to choose a reporter to present its finding at a general information sharing to be conducted an hour later.
- Each unit's representative writes the unit's entire results on a sheet paper, which is presented at the general meeting.

3 **Information sharing: one hour**

Each unit's representative presents its groups' findings at the general meeting.

Meeting leader provides some major categories in which all the data from all the sheets can be classified. E.g. If there are 100 items, the possibility is that these can be classified into 8–9 groups involving heading such as communication difficulties, problem with top management, etc.

The entire group engages itself in a 15-min general session with the meeting leader to go through the raw data on the sheets and assign a category number to each element of data.

4   Priority setting and group action planning: one hour or more

- People assemble in their functional natural work units in for one or more hours.
- Each unit is assigned three specific tasks.
- It is required to discuss the problems and issues, which influence its areas of work, and to ascertain the priorities and early actions to which the group is willing to commit itself.
- It is required to identify the issues and problems to which the management team should give maximum priority.
- It is required to ascertain as how to communicate the findings of the session to their subordinates.

5   Organizational action plan: two hours

Total group is assembled in a general session.

- Each functional unit reports its commitments and plans to the total group. Reports and enlists the items that its members believe the management team should deal with first.
- Top management is required to react to this list and make commitments for action where needed.
- Each unit is required to share briefly its plan for communicating the results of the confrontation meeting to all subordinates.

6   Immediate follow-up: 1–3 hours

Top management team is required to meet immediately after the completion of the confrontation meeting to plan first a set of follow-up action which is to be reported ultimately back to the total management group within a few days.

7   Progress review

After specific intervals progress review of the confrontation meeting is to be taken by the top management team.

Appendix C
Rapid relationality process

Phase 1: rapidly getting in. Peripheral expert gains access to line manager and core knowledge by addressing managers' concerns upfront. "You may have some concerns about..." "It may take some time for me to establish credibility and get your trust but I intend to be core contributor." Another way is to be vouched for by someone who is already a member of the core team. If you do not have anyone you might have to develop a relationship with the most accessible member of the core team first and have them introduce you to the senior leader.

Phase 2: rapidly proving oneself. Peripheral expert gains line manager's trust by making a commitment gesture. Which could mean being responsive. Calling back or texting immediately at or least the same day. If it's after hours call and leave a message. If you go out of your way, they respond to that. It could mean putting in extra hours, being willing to try things a different way first and letting the manager take credit. The expert must also maintain the existing boundaries of authority. Do not try to go around the lines of authority to get things done.

Phase 3: continuously using relational expertise. Peripheral expert minimizes the threat posed and maintains influence by affirming the line managers' authority and supporting the line managers' culture. One way is strategic framing and tapping into the cultural values and schemas most cherished by the dominant group. Go formal until you're invited to go informal and observe how others act around the leader. Do they open the door for them? Offered to get them coffee? Most women understand the meaning of getting coffee for a man and may wish to avoid it. However it is a quick way to bypass any hidden concerns about roles. Look up the acronyms so you can be in the know. Use the word *recommendation* rather than we must do that. Let the line manager be the manager. They are making the decisions for that situation. You can say, "I'm sorry it's a tough call. What's your decision?"

Index

Note: **Bold** page numbers refer to tables; *italic* page numbers refer to figures.

accountability 9–10
Acosta, M. 108
Alloway, T. 20
Ambrose 93
Anjum, Z. 21
Appelbaum 57
Arab Spring 91
Argyris, C. 106
authentically inclusive leadership 3, 8–13
autonomy 102

Barsade, S. 48–49
Batt 57
Beckhard, Richard 111, 115
Beer, M. 70, 87
belonging: expansion of 15–16, *16*; getting to *128*, 127–136; identity and 55–59; leadership and 130–131; power and 56–57; psychological safety and *16*, 26, 102; status and 56–57; *see also* diversity, equity, inclusion and belonging (DEIB)
benchmarking 84–87
Bennis, Warren 3, 88, 96
Bhopal disaster 34–36
biases 28–29, 39
Birmingham, K. 24
Black Lives Matter (BLM) 1–2, 8, 25
BLM *see* Black Lives Matter (BLM)
Böll, M. M. 4, 61, 63
Bourdieu 68
Brooks, Heidi 43
Brown, B. 109
burnout 33–34, 45–46, **46**, 48–49, 83
Byrd, M. Y. 49

C&A *see* Certainty & Agreement (C&A) framework
candid expression, risks of 98–101, *99*, **100**
Capehart, J. 134
Carrillo, R. A. 87, 117
Carsten, B. 69
case study 15
Certainty & Agreement (C&A) framework 77–80, *78*
Chaney, M. P. 38
change management: Certainty & Agreement (C&A) framework in 77–80, *78*; change as nonlinear 75–76; complexity model in 77–80, *78*; conversation in 76; executive level involvement in 81–83; interactive communication and 81; leadership and 14; learning and 88–92, *90*; organizational improvement initiatives and 87–88; organizational transformation and 80–84, *82*; people-centered 75–94, *78*, *82*, *90*; planning and 75–76
change opportunities 29–30
Chernobyl 66–67
child care 23
Chisholm, Shirley 134–135
Clare, J. 24
Clark, T. 33
classism *38*, 38–41, **40**
Coch, L. 24
commitment 14
communication 10–11; bridges 109–110; fear of social interaction and 100–101; interactive 81; open 14; social identity and 88

compassion 48–49
complexity: human social systems and 53–55
complex responsive processes (CRP) 13, 53–54, 76
confrontation meeting 139–140
connectedness 14
Conner, J. 60
consensus 77
conversation: as change mechanism 76
core business identity 122–125, **124**
Covid-19 pandemic 1–2, 8–9, 19–22, 28, 41, 44–48, **46,** 120–121, **121,** *122*
Cross, N. 62
CRP *see* complex responsive processes (CRP)
culture: of compassion 48–49; culture and power 56–57; resignations and 21–22; social identity and 57–58; toxic culture 21–22, 120–121
Cushen 57

Damasio, A. 60
Daniels, I. David. 36, 41–42
Davis, Viola 108
Dean, J. 27
DEIB *see* diversity, equity, inclusion and belonging (DEIB)
DiBenigno, J. 13, 111, 113–114, 123
disconfirmation 90, *90, 93*
discrimination: gender 37–38; mitigating psychosocial risk of 41–42; as psychosocial hazard 36–41, *38,* **40;** racial 37
diversity: workplace, defined 25
diversity, equity, inclusion and belonging (DEIB) 2–3; change management and 91–92; implementation and effectiveness 25–29; initiatives falling short 26–27; *see also* belonging; inclusion
Dobbin, F. 26
Dooley 76
Duhigg, C. 82, 96

EAPs *see* Employee Assistance Plans (EAPs)
Edmondson, Amy 3–4, 26, 76, 96
Eisenhower, Dwight 75
Emery, F. 65
emotion, as language 60–61
emotional culture of compassion 48–49
Employee Assistance Plans (EAPs) 26
empowerment 57

enactment 135–136
engagement 77
equity 102
ethic of responsibility 122
expectations, role of in organizational outcomes 61–62, 66

face, losing 100
failure 77
Fani, N. 36
fear, of social interaction 100–101
French, J. R. 114

Garasic, M. D. 19
gender discrimination 37–38
generative social fields (GSFs) 4, 15, 63–64
Gittell, J. H. 13, 53, 56, 61
Gladwell, Malcolm 86
Goffman, Erving 98
Great Resignation 2, 21–25, *23,* 29–30, 45
Green, John 123–124
GSFs *see* generative social fields (GSFs)

Hall, Tom 64
Hanh, Thich Nhat 48
Harris, R. T. 115
Hatfield, S. 24, 46, 61
Hawley, L. 38
health and safety: advisor 119–122, **121,** *122;* advisor identity 123–124; leadership role 125–126; as leadership strategy 117–126, **121,** *122,* **124**
healthcare workers 23–24
Heyhoe, J. 60
Hollnagel, E. 70
Horn, Clinton 64
Howard-Grenville, J. A. 123
human social systems 4; complexity and 53–55; complex responsive processes and 53–54; measuring results in 68–71; organizations in 71; secret life of 52–71, *66;* technical systems and 64–68, *66*
Hutchingson, Georgia Bryce 45
hybrid work 65–66; psychosocial risks with 42–44; *see also* virtual technology (VT)

identity: belonging and 55–59; core business 122–125, **124;** of health and safety advisors 123–124; leadership and 130–131; personal 131; professional 59, 131; *see also* social identity

inclusion: accountability and 9–10; communication and 10–11; defined 25; empowerment and 57; expansion of 15–16, *16*; getting to *128,* 127–136; innovation and 11–12; leadership and 130–131, **137–138**; motivation and 103; philosophy of 8–13; power and 56–57; power of 133–135; psychological safety and *16,* 26, 103–105; resilience and 11–12; status and 56–57; success and 12–13; *see also* diversity, equity, inclusion and belonging (DEIB)
innovation 11–12
interactive communication 81
interdisciplinary conversations 112–113
isolation, in remote work 43

Jacobson, L. 13
joint optimization *66,* 66–67
Josephson, P. R. 66
Jung, Carl 16

Kalev, A. 26
Kapitza, S. P. 66
Kelly, O. C. G. 43, 46
Kennedy, Peggy Wallace 134
Khan 96
Kunz, Bob 8

Lavaza, A. 19
Lawton, R. 60
leadership: authentically inclusive 3, 7–18, *16;* belonging and 130–131; change management and 14; health and safety as strategy for 117–126, **121,** *122,* **124;** identity and 130–131; inclusion and 130–131, **137–138;** servant 29–30; women in *23*
Levenson, N. 65
Lewin, K. 76, 88–90
Lieberman, M. D. 10
Lloyd, C. 37
Lloyd-Jones, B. 37
losing face 100
Loud, J. 65
Luhmann 59
Lynch, Elisa 70

Marinus, James 64, 111–112
Masten, C. L. 36
Matthews, Melissa 46–47
Mellor, S. 21

mental health: Covid-19 and 44–48, **46;** investing in 46–48; mortality and 33–34; psychosocial risk and 33–49, **35,** *38,* **40, 46**
Miller, A. 21

Nonaka, I. 53
Noriah, N. 70

O'Brien, Bill 127
Önday, Ö. 7
O'Neill, Paul 82, 111
open communication 14
organizational improvement initiatives 87–88
organizational outcomes *16*
organizational transformation 80–84, *82*
Orvits. K. 21

Pahountis, Lou 83
Parker, Jim 61
Parsons, Talcott 17, 54–55
PDCA *see* Plan, Do, Check, Act (PDCA)
Pearson, C. 100
Perrow, C. 56
personal identity 55
Plan, Do, Check, Act (PDCA) 125
planning 75–77, 81, 85, 111
political relationships 114–115, **115–116**
Pomeroy, E. 53
Porath, C. 100
positive deviance 83–84
positive inquiry 83
power 56–57
power relations 53
professional identity 59, 131
promotions, of women 23
PS *see* psychological safety (PS)
PSHs *see* psychosocial hazards (PSHs)
psychological safety (PS) 3–4, 7; belonging and *16,* 26, 102; in change process *90,* 90–91; change readiness and 93; core social needs for 102; inclusion and *16,* 26, 103–105; as local 102–103; relationship and 13; responsibility for generation of 97–98; risks of candid expression 98–101, *99,* **100;** value of 96–105, *99,* **100;** *see also* health and safety
psychological stages of change process 89–91, *90*
psychosocial hazards (PSHs): classism as *38,* 38–41, **40;** defined 33; discrimination as 36–41, *38,* **40;**

examples **35**; management and 34–36, **35**; work-related 34
psychosocial risk 33–49, **35**, *38, **40, 46***

race 36
racial discrimination 37
Ramos, M. R. 92
Raven, B. 114
Rea, Joe 86
Reay, T. 85
relational partnership 14–15
relationships: building 10, 13; as foundation of organization 11; performance and 13–14, 106–115, **115–116**; political 114–115, **115–116**; social fields and 62–63
remote work *see* hybrid work; virtual technology (VT)
resilience 11–12
respect 39–41, 102, 104
responsibility, ethic of 122
return-to-office plans 43–44
risk: of candid expression 98–101, *99,* **100**; emotional capacity for interpersonal 108; psychosocial 33–49, **35,** *38,* **40, 46**; resilience and 11–12; social, in employee perspective 101; of social interaction 107–109; social status and 99–100
Rosenthal, R. 13
Rozovsky, J. 53

Saad, L. 43
safety *see* health and safety; psychological safety (PS)
Scharmer, O. 53, 63, 127
Schein, Edgar 3, 65, 86, 88–89, 91, 96
Schein, P. A. 65
Schon, D. 106
Schrader, D. 87
security 102
self-accountability 10
self-efficacy *16*
self-inquiry 16–18
Senge, P. 4, 63–64
servant leadership 29–30
Shannon, C. E. 37
Shorrock, S. 107
Snowden, Dave 53, 59
social fields 59–63; emotion and 60–61; generative 4, 15, 63–64; influencing change from within 61–62; relationships and 62–63

social identity 130; communication and 88; culturally diverse, management of 57–58; dark side of 58–59; theory 55
socialization, of technology 67–68
social needs 102
social systems, human *see* human social systems
sociotechnical systems 65–67, *66*
Spataro, Jared 21
Stacey, Ralph 53, 75–77
Stacey's Matrix 78, *78*
status 56–57, 99–100; *see also* classism
Sternin, Jerry 84
Stettiner, Bill 19–20
Stevens, Cameron 67–68
Sull, D. 21
survival anxiety 90, *90,* 93
Sutcliffe, K. 34

Tajfel, H. 55
Takeuchi, H. 53
teachers 24
teams: high-performance *16*
technology socialization 67–68
terminology 2–6
toxic culture 21–22, 120–121
Trevino, J. A. 98
Trist, E. L. 65
Trump, Donald 91
trust 10–11, 113–114

uncertainty 77

Van Kleef, G. A. 60
Vietnam 84
virtual technology (VT) 20–21; *see also* hybrid work
voice 131–133
VT *see* virtual technology (VT)

Wade, Kenneth 120
Waldrop 76
Walker, T. 24, 30
Weick, Karl 34–35, 69, 135
Weisenthal, J. 20
Wheatley 76
Wigert, B. 43
Wiles, J. 21
women 22–24, *23,* 37–38, 45–46, **46**
work from home 20–21; *see also* hybrid work

Yong, E. 24

Zohar, D. 53

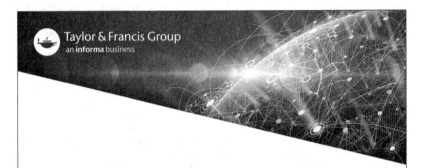

Printed in the United States
by Baker & Taylor Publisher Services